ROUTLEDGE LIBRARY EDITIONS:
LIBRARY AND INFORMATION SCIENCE

Volume 56

MANAGEMENT ISSUES IN THE NETWORKING ENVIRONMENT

MANAGEMENT ISSUES IN THE NETWORKING ENVIRONMENT

Edited by
EDWARD R. JOHNSON

LONDON AND NEW YORK

First published in 1988 by The Haworth Press, Inc.

This edition first published in 2020
by Routledge
2 Park Square, Milton Park, Abingdon, Oxon OX14 4RN

and by Routledge
52 Vanderbilt Avenue, New York, NY 10017

Routledge is an imprint of the Taylor & Francis Group, an informa business

© 1988 The Haworth Press, Inc.

All rights reserved. No part of this book may be reprinted or reproduced or utilised in any form or by any electronic, mechanical, or other means, now known or hereafter invented, including photocopying and recording, or in any information storage or retrieval system, without permission in writing from the publishers.

Trademark notice: Product or corporate names may be trademarks or registered trademarks, and are used only for identification and explanation without intent to infringe.

British Library Cataloguing in Publication Data
A catalogue record for this book is available from the British Library

ISBN: 978-0-367-34616-4 (Set)
ISBN: 978-0-429-34352-0 (Set) (ebk)
ISBN: 978-0-367-42294-3 (Volume 56) (hbk)
ISBN: 978-0-367-42295-0 (Volume 56) (pbk)
ISBN: 978-0-367-82325-2 (Volume 56) (ebk)

Publisher's Note
The publisher has gone to great lengths to ensure the quality of this reprint but points out that some imperfections in the original copies may be apparent.

Disclaimer
The publisher has made every effort to trace copyright holders and would welcome correspondence from those they have been unable to trace.

Management Issues in the Networking Environment

Edward R. Johnson
Editor

The Haworth Press
New York • London

Management Issues in the Networking Environment has also been published as *Journal of Library Administration*, Volume 8, Numbers 3/4, Fall/Winter 1987.

© 1988 by The Haworth Press, Inc. All rights reserved. No part of this work may be reproduced or utilized in any form or by any means, electronic or mechanical, including photocopying, microfilm, and recording, or by any information storage and retrieval system, without permission in writing from the publisher. Printed in the United States of America.

The Haworth Press, Inc., 12 West 32 Street, New York, NY 10001
EUROSPAN/Haworth, 3 Henrietta Street, London WC2E 8LU England

LIBRARY OF CONGRESS
Library of Congress Cataloging-in-Publication Data

Management issues in the networking environment / Edward R. Johnson, editor.
   p. cm.
  Published also as Journal of library administration, vol. 8, nos. 3/4, fall/winter 1987.
  Includes bibliographical references.
  ISBN 0-86656-692-9
  1. Library information networks—United States—Management. 2. Library administration—United States. 3. Libraries—United States—Automation—Management. I. Johnson, Edward R.
Z674.8.M36 1987
021.6'5'068—dc19
                                                                           87-32940
                                                                                CIP

Management Issues in the Networking Environment

CONTENTS

NEWS AND CALENDAR *Coy L. Harmon*	1
Introduction *Edward R. Johnson*	5
Management Perspectives on Network Membership *Thomas W. Shaughnessy*	7

PART I: CURRENT NETWORKING PROBLEMS AND PROSPECTS

The Issues and Needs of a Local Library Consortium *Edward M. Walters*	15

The purpose of this paper is to develop definitions and a model for networking, a field in which terminology is not always clear. One reason for this, in the author's view, is that local consortium identity is so closely tied up with a broader "culture" of library collaboration. Several needs are identified that the local consortium needs to address in order to continue being effective.

Multistate Library Networks: A Model for Lay Representation on Library Network Boards *Louella V. Wetherbee*	31

This paper reviews the organization of governing boards of multistate library networks and proposes a model for lay representation on such boards. The author reviews the roles and responsibilities of network boards. She concludes that participation by lay members in network governance strengthens the effectiveness of networks and helps give members greater participation in the decision-making process.

Vision and Reality: The Research Libraries and Networking 51
      Paul M. Gherman

   This article looks at the changing attitudes of research libraries toward
   multitype, regional, and national bibliographic networks as technology, local agendas, and economics change. Research libraries, according to the author, are more likely to cooperate out of self-interest
   than from "apple pie and motherhood" type sentiments. The development of local systems and local area networks will absorb their full
   attention.

Networking and Institutional Planning 59
      Donald E. Riggs

   Network participation requires that libraries pay more attention to a
   formal planning process in decision-making. The author suggests that
   it is necessary for the institutional mission statement and the library's
   stated goals to be compatible and to incorporate more objectives relating to issues such as access and cooperation. Strategies are suggested
   to help libraries plan for future directions in networking.

Ownership of Bibliographic Data and Its Importance to Consortia 69
      Charles B. Lowry

   This topic was of little concern to libraries a few years ago but is now
   of considerable importance. In this article the author analyzes the
   sometimes conflicting issues of protecting bibliographic databases
   while safeguarding access to information for individual library use.
   The fundamentally different approaches to record ownership and use
   by the various bibliographic utilities are discussed. An argument is
   made for improved contractual agreements between libraries, consortia, and networks rather than copyright registration.

The Future of Networks and OCLC 85
      Irene B. Hoadley

   The history of the relationship between OCLC and the regional networks is traced in this article. In an attempt to determine if this relationship will continue in the future the author examines current stresses
   and discusses possible alternatives. She concludes that OCLC and the
   networks must continue to be partners if their member libraries are not
   to suffer a loss of service.

PART II: THE FUTURE OF NETWORKING

Library Networking: Statement of a Common Vision 93
      Library of Congress Network Advisory Committee

   This summary of the Network Advisory Committee's stance on networking was used as a point of discussion in a recent joint conference of two
   regional bibliographic networks—AMIGOS and SOLINET.

Toward a Nationwide Library Network 95
  Henriette D. Avram

In this paper the author traces the development of library networking over the last twenty years. She expresses concern regarding the present library environment. Many libraries are emphasizing local systems and no longer seem to subscribe to the community's earlier goal of an integrated national network. The political and economic problems of the Linked Systems Project are discussed as well as issues relating to copyright.

Strategies for Networking in the Next Ten Years 117
  D. Kaye Gapen

In response to the paper by Avram, the author has another view of networking. This paper addresses a perception of networking in which its future remains intact. Future networking prospects are hopeful, in the author's view, if frustrating. Strategies for networking are provided.

Balancing Needs: The Ideal Network of the Future 131
  Susan K. Martin

This paper is also in response to Avram's paper. The author shares a concern with the direction that local systems development is taking libraries. In particular the changing entrepreneurial character of OCLC and the regional networks is discussed. She concludes that networks will have to think more like businesses in the future.

NEWS AND CALENDAR

As this special issue of the *Journal of Library Administration* appears, the question of who will succeed Daniel Boorstin as Librarian of Congress will have been resolved. For a while, however, there was considerable debate in the library world over whether Boorstin's replacement should be a librarian or a "scholar." There were many who suggested that a scholarly librarian should not be too difficult to find.

That politics is a game to be played in the selection of a new Librarian of Congress is an accepted fact. However, reports that President Reagan was having difficulty in locating a qualified candidate who was also a librarian forced a few wrinkles in the face of U.S. librarianship. Some library groups offered to assist President Reagan by nominating or suggesting candidates for the LC position.

Daniel Boorstin served his post well and was a good example of a Librarian of Congress who learned how to fulfill his mission to Congress and to serve the citizens of the United States as well. Librarian or not, Boorstin's replacement will be successful only if he or she understands the complex, multi-dimensional role of the Library of Congress, is committed to the basic library principle of the right to access information, and is capable of identifying qualified colleagues and delegating to them the responsibility and authority to carry out the many functions of the Library of Congress.

Will the change in leadership at LC have an impact on the management of libraries across the country? It is hard to tell at this point, but since most libraries are tied in somehow to the functions and processes of LC, a new Librarian of Congress with new ideas or programs could easily set off a minor ripple that could become a tidal wave to the library community.

Has Mr. Meese or one of his followers been to your library yet? The disappearance of *Playboy* and *Penthouse* from thousands of stores across the country shows that the Meese Commission on Pornography

---

Coy L. Harmon is Dean of Libraries at Murray State University, Murray, KY.

© 1988 by The Haworth Press, Inc. All rights reserved.

did more than simply create a report (LJ January 1987). Many people who would like to impose their tastes in reading on everyone else are using the Meese Report to systematically remove selected books and journals from the shelves.

While some librarians may not be too concerned about what happens to commercial establishments, censorship of printed materials will not stop there. Organized pressure on libraries will grow, and public libraries will be particularly vulnerable to the criticisms leveled by a few overzealous community members who will be thumping their Meese "Bibles."

The best defense against censorship is the availability of a clearly defined collection development policy which has been endorsed by the library's governing agency. Since most censorship attempts will come from a member or members of the library's service community, it is also advisable to identify and enlist the aid of other community leaders who share the library's view on the rights of choice and who support the library's collection development program.

The issue of censorship should not become a conflict between the library and its community. It is a community matter in which the library must participate, and it must strongly emphasize its role in serving the entire community based on the time-honored principles of the freedom of choice, the freedom to read and the right to access information.

Through the pages of library literature over a period of just a few months, we witnessed the strange and sometimes unbelievable events which befell Olin Library at Washington University in St. Louis. The resignation of Charles D. Churchwell as library dean was prompted by the decision of University Vice-Chancellor Rosett to accept and implement the recommendations of the consulting firm Alexander Proudfoot Company of Chicago. Although the firm reportedly had never before had a library as a client (AL March 1987), and even though there was strong resistance to the company's recommendations on the part of the library administration, the proposal to reduce the library staff by one-third and implement many other procedures normally foreign to an academic library was submitted and accepted. With Churchwell gone and several other library staffers dismissed or reassigned, life in Olin Library became somewhat unbearable for some.

In March of this year a petition signed by a majority of library employees resulted in an administrative review of the situation. Proudfoot was asked to leave the library, and the head of the law library was appointed as acting dean reporting directly to the provost instead of Vice-Chancellor Rosett. Rosett subsequently resigned as Vice-Chancellor and Dean of Faculty but remained on the faculty at Washington University (AL April 1987).

Few people outside the Olin Library and Washington University know what really prompted the events at Olin earlier this year. However, it became immediately apparent that whatever ills, real or imaginary, were to be cured, the library was a unique organization that required diagnostics relevant to its purpose and structure. Libraries in general, and Olin Library in particular, have fallen victim to the scrutiny of those who have little understanding of what a library is or does. As librarians, however, we must share in the responsibility for this situation. Too often we cloak our activities in procedures and terminology known only to us, and what may appear to our public to be a simple job performed in a competent manner may in fact be a complex procedure or service made to look deceptively easy. The library administrator would do well to give his or her supervisor or governing board a behind-the-scenes look at library operations with a full explanation of how the various processes and activities evolve into a system of services for the library's patrons.

Is it simply a case of "what goes around comes around"? In *College: The Undergraduate Experience in America*, a 1986 report issued by the Carnegie Foundation for the Advancement of Teaching, we find the conclusion that there is a general lack of use of the campus library by students. The report further states that one out of four students never use the library, and 65% use it four hours or less each week.

If this sounds familiar, it should. A Carnegie report issued fifty years ago arrived at the same basic conclusions. The findings of the report may not be new to us, but an analysis of the reasons behind the findings should be the subject of another report. While we may fault students for not using the library on their own initiative, it is too often the case that teaching faculty and classroom expectations do not require the use of the library. It is a sad commentary on our system of higher education that many faculty teach from a limited number of textbooks and never require their students to investigate resources outside the classroom.

What's in a name? The ongoing debate over the naming of libraries and library schools is both serious and amusing. A name should reflect the nature of a function, but while we argue and muse over words, we may be in danger of losing sight of the most fundamental components of our profession including library education and service. Virtually every issue of the major library journals has some statement of yet another library school closing or of one coming under the close scrutiny of budget trimmers at one of our universities. The problem may not yet be critical, but the profession could be faced with a severe shortage of qualified librarians in a few years.

Along with the problem of where librarians should be educated, library administrators and educators must work together to address the problem of how librarians will be educated. Satisfactory resolutions to the very serious problems of library school closings and the design of library education in this country will require the best efforts of all of us.

With the announcement earlier this year that RLG, OCLC, WLN, and the Library of Congress had reached agreement on several aspects of the Linked Systems Project (LJ February 1, 1987), including protocols for records transfer, many library managers can now contemplate what advantages interagency records transfer and shared cataloging searching may offer to libraries and their patrons. For those still interested in the concept of a national library system, they may be seeing in the Linked Systems Project a little bit of the future.

Although you may still be resting up from the American Library Association Annual Conference which was held in San Francisco, it is time to start planning for upcoming events. Some of you may have made it to the General Conference of the International Federation of Library Associations and Institutions held in Brighton, U.K., August 16-22, 1987. Perhaps you stayed closer to home and attended the Annual Conference of the American Society for Information Science which was held in Boston, October 4-9, 1987.

The Midwinter Meeting of the American Library Association is moving south to San Antonio, Texas for the week of January 9-14, 1988. The Annual Conference of ALA will be held in New Orleans, July 9-14, 1988. The Special Libraries Association will be visiting historic Williamsburg, Virginia for its winter meeting to be held January 27-29, and its Annual Conference will take place in Denver the week of June 11-16, 1988.

Coy L. Harmon

Introduction

Recently, Michael Gorman (apparently with tongue partially in cheek) opined that "cooperation is not an activity that libraries may or may not choose to engage in—it is the element in which they live and prosper. Cooperation is as essential to a library as is water to a fish or air to a mammal."[1]

While Gorman may have deliberately overstated the situation somewhat to make a point, many library administrators are spending a higher percentage of their time on interlibrary cooperative programs. The reason for this expenditure of time and energy is that libraries today must share their resources because they are no longer able, if indeed they ever were, to afford the building of stand-alone research level collections, staffing, and services to support all academic fields. Also, the high cost of technology and its rapid change are driving libraries to seek ways to share the costs of development while also sharing the benefits.

A major question facing academic library administrators such as myself is how to develop and improve interinstitutional cooperation. "Networking" these days can mean anything from establishing friendships, to implementing local area computer networks, to working with regional or local library consortia. For the purpose of this issue, the term "networking" is used in a broad sense in order to encompass the many activities that libraries are engaged in for interlibrary cooperation.

As those who have been engaged in such activities know only too well, there are many concerns (which I have chosen to call "management issues" in this edition) facing library administrators trying to administer such networks. As the reader will soon discover there is no consensus regarding the characteristics and goals of networks. Further, networking is characterized by considerable discussion as to governance, planning, economic and legal problems, leadership needs, appropriate products and services, and the resolution of political concerns.

In my own experience, once decision-making moves beyond the

local library level, a number of concerns and possible obstacles to interlibrary cooperation are encountered. For example, university administrators must operate in a highly-charged political environment and they are particularly sensitive to outside commitments and involvements on the part of their institution. While publicly very supportive of interlibrary cooperative programs, privately they have reservations about the need for reliance on other institutions, giving up autonomy, and the cost, benefits, and feasibility of such commitments.

In addition to such problems, events of recent years have shown that information (previously regarded as mostly free and to be disseminated among libraries on the basis of hand-shake deals) has become a valuable commodity. OCLC management, for instance, understood the value of this commodity and thus undertook to copyright the online union catalog much to the surprise and unhappiness of many librarians. The resultant debate demonstrates just how much the environment for library administrators has changed in recent years and why networking has become so complex.

Despite such problems and concerns library networks continue to grow and to expand. Predicting the future is chancy but it seems certain that such cooperation will continue. Library administrators for the most part recognize that the future increasingly will involve greater interinstitutional commitments. They also know that they will have to educate, persuade, explain, and convince their bosses that such resource-sharing programs and activities are politically desirable, economically sound, and beneficial to the library's clientele.

The purpose of this issue, then, is to identify some of the problems and prospects facing library administrators in the networking environment. The following papers address these management issues from a number of different viewpoints. All the authors have had extensive experience in networking activities and their observations and ideas should be valuable contributions to the literature on the subject.

Edward R. Johnson

NOTE

1. Michael Gorman, "Laying Siege to the 'Fortress Library,'" *American Libraries*, 17 (May, 1986), p. 325.

Management Perspectives on Network Membership

Thomas W. Shaughnessy

Although libraries in the United States do not constitute a major industry (expenditures for materials and binding in 1983-84 totalled only $1.3 billion), this outlay is sufficient to support a variety of service industries. These include book and periodical jobbers, companies which provide for the retrospective conversion of bibliographic records, those which provide authority control, and brokers for various data base services. Typically, a symbiotic relationship exists between the jobber and the library. We need them, for example, to facilitate the acquisition of foreign publications, to consolidate and simplify record-keeping and billing, and to expedite purchases and claims. And they need us, obviously, for our business.

There is, naturally, a charge for these services. The costs vary from jobber to jobber, and are typically calculated as a percentage of the dollar value of the business given a particular company. The more money spent with a jobber, the lower the service fee, and/or the higher the discount on materials or services purchased.

Many library managers believe that the services provided by jobbers and other middlemen are well worth the additional cost. Many approval plan vendors are able to save money for their clients by offering discounts which are larger than those normally available to libraries. Managers also tend to believe that the costs of additional library staff to provide the services offered by jobbers would exceed by far the costs of purchasing these services. It is not at all certain, however, that cost/benefit studies have been carried out on this question.

The purpose of this paper is to examine only one of these service agencies—the library network—from the perspective of library management. By "network" is meant one of the 20 or so organizations which broker the services of bibliographic utilities or other data bases.

While there is great diversity among networks, most provide certain

---

Thomas W. Shaughnessy is Director of Libraries at the University of Missouri-Columbia.

basic services. These include training and consultation, billing, technical services and communications relative to the products and services of one or more bibliographic utilities. In addition, some networks offer services such as microcomputer support, document delivery, contract cataloging, union lists of serials, access to on-line reference data bases, electronic mail, collection analysis based on classification counts, discounts on hardware and supplies, and storage and maintenance of computer tapes. A few networks are beginning to explore possible roles with respect to facilitating reciprocal borrowing and the preservation of library resources.

Networks are also distinguished by the size of their membership (from about 20 to more than 3000 members), territory covered (single state, multi-state, or restricted to libraries which are agencies of the federal government), type of governance structure, financing, and their relationships with similar entities such as state libraries.

Network staffs vary in size from two to more than 50 employees, with the average network employing 16 staff. It is estimated that approximately 7,000 libraries in the U.S. belong to networks, either as full, partial or affiliated members.

Networks whose service areas are limited to the boundaries of a particular state may or may not be associated with their state libraries. Some function as agencies of state government and are supported by state appropriations, while others are quite independent and receive no state support. Yet oftentimes the goals of state libraries with respect to fostering interlibrary cooperation and resource sharing coincide very closely with those of networks. One wonders why more coordination and cooperation do not exist even in those cases where networks are not formally associated with state libraries.

Based on this overview of their organization and services, it is evident that networks are providing important services to their clients. There is clearly a need for the kinds of services offered, since so many libraries have joined the networks. Nor can one argue with their goals and objectives. After all, organizations which encourage interlibrary cooperation are valued in our profession.

Despite the accomplishments of networks and the many services they provide, it is not uncommon to find that library administrators are quite concerned about them and their libraries' role in them. Areas of greatest concern are first, the costs of participation; second, network governance; and third, interagency relationships.

COST OF NETWORK PARTICIPATION

Each network typically charges an annual membership fee of several hundred dollars. These funds are normally used to cover costs associated with network publications and some office overhead. Most of a network's operating capital is generated from fees for service, that is, a percentage surcharge on all of the services brokered by the network, and cost recovery fees (for example, those charged for workshops and site visits).

Additional revenue is frequently generated from interest earned on prepaid accounts. Many libraries prefer to estimate their annual network service charges and prepay the entire amount at the beginning of the fiscal year. This large influx of cash enables the network to weather all of the cash-flow problems which sometimes characterize membership organizations. But more importantly, it provides the network with interest income. Prepaid accounts also help the network reduce those costs associated with billing and bookkeeping. Because of the many advantages associated with prepaid accounts, networks provide a discount of a few percentage points to encourage this practice. For larger libraries, this discount may result in some sizeable savings. Prepayment also protects the library from unanticipated midyear budget cuts.

Every organization has its "dead-beats," and networks, unfortunately, are no exception. Occasionally, member accounts fall 60 to 90 or more days in arrears. In fact, some institutions seem to have adopted a "slow-pay" policy. They operate about a quarter-year behind in terms of bill payment. This practice enables them to spread their costs beyond the fiscal year. While penalties are sometimes assessed by the networks, many institutions tend to ignore them. Some, in fact, are not able legally to pay such penalties.

One outcome of this situation is that the membership fees and prepaid accounts of some members are being used to carry the debt of other members. Library managers who prepay their network charges may speculate whether their service discounts would not be significantly larger were their funds not used by the network as a cash flow cushion.

Because networks are recognized by purchasing officers as legitimate service vendors, they can sometimes be used by library directors to "hide" budgeted funds. If a library were to receive, for example, a large amount of unanticipated funding which had to be spent by the end of the fiscal year, it might deposit the funds with its network. The funds could then be expended to prepay network charges, to purchase equipment and supplies through the network, or for other library purposes — all without the end of fiscal year deadline. However, library managers should not use their networks to circumvent local purchasing regulations or bid processes. While such collusion between a network director and library administrators may be quite legal, it does tend to co-opt individual members of the network.

NETWORK GOVERNANCE AND PRIORITIES

A second area of concern for library managers is the governance of networks and resulting priorities. All networks are governed by a board of directors elected, for the most part, from the membership. Each member library has one vote, but is represented throughout the year by board members who make policy and budgetary decisions. Typically, the network's executive director is ex officio a member of the board.

One problem inherent in this structure is the conflicting priorities of large and small libraries. Larger libraries typically look to their networks for brokerage services. Smaller libraries which do not use bibliographic utilities or search commercial or other data bases use other network services: staff training and consultation, interlibrary loan, etc. This conflict is perhaps best illustrated by the organization of at least one "no-frills" network which has a very small staff and only offers brokerage service to a bibliographic utility. The fact is that even when a network charges additional fees for staff-intensive services, it rarely recovers the total cost of delivering those services. This means that those libraries which neither need nor want such services are subsidizing services to other member libraries. The more the network relies on brokerage service charges to support its operation, the greater the subsidy.

In any network, smaller libraries will outnumber the larger library members. This is true with respect to most of the various networks which currently exist and with respect to all of the utilities except for RLIN. The so-called tyranny of the majority which is inherent in network governance led OCLC to establish a forum for larger research-oriented libraries. This organization, called RLAC, is now in its seventh year, and has proved to be a very effective mechanism for addressing the interests of larger libraries. A similar organization developed within the AMIGOS network in 1979. This organization, named CARL (Council of Amigos Research Libraries), performs the same function.

Larger libraries are sometimes viewed as big fish in small ponds. Their library administrators are sometimes frustrated by their limited voice (one vote per member) in network affairs, even though their financial support of the network is very disproportionate. And to the extent that networks provide services to nonmembers of the network, their tolerance for such inequity is strained even further.

But perhaps the most significant area of conflict between large and smaller members is just beginning to emerge. The availability of bibliographic records on CD-ROM has already caused some smaller libraries to cancel their relationship with OCLC and their network membership. This is viewed as a real challenge by the networks, and they are currently searching for ways to serve the smaller library which cannot pay for (and perhaps does not need) OCLC services. One problem in attempting to meet this challenge is that providing individual libraries with an inexpensive method for converting their bibliographic records does not necessarily lead to transferring those records to a statewide or regional data base. In other words, the processing of bibliographic records is not the same as developing systems for resource sharing.

Yet despite these difficulties, most library managers must be impressed with the calibre of network directors. Most of the networks have been very successful in attracting strong, well-qualified executive directors. Not only are these individuals fine managers, but they are also accomplished teachers and facilitators. Given the character and high quality of this group, library managers should expect them to be entrepreneurs, to develop their organizations, and to build empires. The challenge for the director of a member library (who may or may not be a member of the network board) is to strike a balance between encouraging the creativity and energy of the network director while at the same time calling attention to limits of growth and the fact that membership priorities may not always coincide with those of the network's director. Ambiguities inherent in network by-laws on the one hand, and the relaxed attention of board members on the other, can create situations in which the network director assumes far more autonomy and authority than membership would want.

There are other situations in which the interests of member libraries might conflict with those of the network. It is conceivable that a network might preempt a library's application for grant funds, for example. In other situations, the network director might sit on a proposal reviewing panel, and experience conflicting sentiments. And finally, the responsibility of, say, OCLC networks to market OCLC products and services might cause the network to recommend a product which is not as well suited to a particular installation as a competing product is. In this situation, the network's goals (to market a particular product) may take precedence over the member library's interests.

But perhaps the most sensitive area for possible conflict of interest is the networks' position with respect to negotiating a new contract with OCLC. Various drafts of the new contract were shared with the OCLC Users Council, which is comprised of network representatives. And while the Users Council has played an extremely important and beneficial role in improving the contract, library managers must take care that network interests (whatever they may be) are not represented as being entirely the same as the interests of member libraries. The understandable network preoccupation of OCLC networks with the question, "Is there life after OCLC?," is not a pressing issue in the minds of most library managers. So long as networks continue to provide essential services and meet the needs of their members, it seems safe to assume that they will continue to play an important role and enjoy the support of their members.

INTERAGENCY RELATIONSHIPS

Library managers are often astounded by the number of agencies within a region which are trying to do the same thing. Continuing education or staff development is a good example. Not only are library networks plowing this field, but so are state library agencies, various library associations, library schools, on-line users groups, library consortia, commercial organizations and individual libraries. The library profession's concern with continuing education is certainly praiseworthy, but the effort is too often characterized by fragmentation, duplication, and occasional lapses in quality.

As brokers of on-line services, networks have some responsibility for the training of staff in member libraries. It is, after all, in both the members' and the network's interests for the brokered services to be used as efficiently and effectively as possible. Network staff who provide this training are typically accomplished teachers who know their subject very, very well. In view of their qualifications and grasp of the new technology, it is understandable for network staff to tend to expand their purview to include a wide range of microcomputer support to member libraries. It is at this point where the question is raised whether such broad gauge training is properly the mission of network staff. The question, however, has become all the more complicated with the advent of the OCLC M-300 terminals. These machines can be used as personal computers when they are not on-line with OCLC.

Should not the networks assist libraries in using this equipment for data base management, word processing, accounting, and other purposes?

Relationships between state library agencies and networks often tend to be ambiguous, except in those situations in which the state library provides network services. Both organizations have very similar missions. However, networks typically have more autonomy than state library agencies and are able to respond to service needs very promptly. From an organizational perspective, they frequently have the flexibility to adapt to changing technologies more quickly than their members. This capacity on the one hand, and the entrepreneurial instincts of network directors on the other, occasionally give networks a role as change-agents vis-a-vis their members. There is nothing wrong with this, just so long as all parties are aware of what is happening.

Library managers are usually suspicious of "single-source" vendors. They seek the best buy for the dollar, and give their business to the company which has the most competitive prices. It is not easy to practice this policy with respect to network services, however. Each network, with perhaps one or two exceptions, has a recognized service area. It serves the libraries within its region and does not seek to enlist members from other regions. One reason for this is that larger service areas require larger network staffs, and result in increased travel and communication costs. But an unfortunate result of this situation is that it eliminates competition among the networks and hinders libraries from shopping for network services.

The close ties that exist among networks have been reinforced by the drawn out contract negotiations with OCLC. An unfortunate "us (the networks) against them (OCLC)" attitude has sometimes been evidenced, and this has strengthened inter-network relationships.

Relations between networks and library systems within networks have not always been as harmonious as they might be. Occasionally, there may be confusion in the mind of an administrator whose library holds membership in a local system as well as in a network. If both, for example, provide interlibrary loan service, or cataloging date (from different sources), or inservice training (to name but a few services), one or the other may perceive an infringement on its "territory." It is interesting to note, however, that this would not likely occur among networks because they have taken pains to protect each other's turf! While it is no doubt true that there is room for everybody in this environment, library managers may sometimes puzzle whether such overlap and fragmentation serve their libraries as efficiently as possible.

FUTURE DIRECTIONS

The many uncertainties which confront library administrators on a daily basis also confront their network counterparts. Anxieties caused by the pace of technological change, the shifting priorities of member libraries, and the rise in competition in every form serve to compound the challenge for network directors. OCLC, itself, admits to being "unsure that past relationships will continue to serve all of its interests."[1]

To the extent that individual libraries have a stake in their networks, their administrators need to become more informed and involved in network development. Library managers need to assist the networks in wrestling with questions such as the wisdom of putting all of their eggs in, say, the OCLC basket. What will be the effects of a myriad of off-line products on network membership? What role might networks play in linking local systems? Will the market for network services become so differentiated that larger libraries seek only off-line network services and products? How might networks plan to meet these challenges?

Each library administrator will view such questions differently. An administrator's first concern, naturally, must be the success of his or her own library. To the extent that such success (as measured by program effectiveness, the efficiency with which services are delivered, and unit costs) depends on participation in networks, the motivation for library management's concern and involvement in network governance is there. But library administrators must seek to maintain a high degree of objectivity, lest their concern for the network's viability and success weaken their commitment to their local organizations. In other words, dispassionate judgment is essential. In the last analysis, library administrators must seek out the most economical sources of products and services and the most cost-effective solutions to problems. And while networks are important providers at this stage in the evolution of the electronic library, it is by no means certain that they will play such a role indefinitely.

NOTE

1. Roland C. W. Brown, *OCLC: Present Issues, Future Directions*. (Dublin, Ohio: OCLC, 1985), p. 3.

PART I:
CURRENT NETWORKING PROBLEMS AND PROSPECTS

The Issues and Needs of a Local Library Consortium

Edward M. Walters

PROBLEMS OF DEFINITION

A difficult problem confronting anyone who attempts to clarify the issues and needs of a local library consortium is the task of defining a "local library consortium" with sufficient precision to permit accurate and useful generalization about its behavior as a generic institutional form of library collaborative activity or networking. It is an unfortunate condition of social science that the entities our literature characterizes as "library networks," "library consortia," "library associations," "library systems," and "library cooperatives" cannot be studied with the scientific precision of measuring uniform quantities in an environment that is assumed to be uniform. This fact leaves a residue of ambiguity in library thought about networking and its various institutional forms, one of those forms being the local library consor-

---

Edward M. Walters is Director of the McDermott Library of the University of Texas at Dallas. His degrees are: BA in History, Baylor University; MA in History, University of Georgia; PhD in History and MALS, University of Chicago. Walters has been active in the Association for Higher Education of North Texas and recently served a term as Chair of that organization's Library Committee.

© 1988 by The Haworth Press, Inc. All rights reserved.

tium. As has been observed, "without a clear definition of a network, we tend to visualize the network that serves our library or region."[1]

Because an understanding of the local library consortium as an institutional form is a precondition for comprehending its issues, concerns, and present needs, one cannot, as sometimes happens, formally acknowledge, but quickly dispense with, the problems of definition and terminology that accompany discussion of networks and consortia. In fact, it is a theme of this paper that the inability to define a local consortium adequately has contributed to the condition of its having a tangled identity, and that this tangled identity may result in the consortium having an unclear role, scope, and mission, may inhibit the formulation of effective criteria and standards for measuring program activity, and may lead to the organizational condition that thoughtful managers fear—a self-perpetuating form that is without purpose, organized means directed toward unclear ends, and an empty formalism and mechanistic ritual that is without substance and conviction.

PURPOSE

It is the purpose of this paper, then, to define a local library consortium as a generic institutional form of library collaborative activity, to clarify the role that local library consortia play in the context of a national "network culture," to identify some of the primary belief systems that sustain the local consortia, and finally, to highlight the issues and needs of local consortia in the contemporary environment of library collaboration.

The initial problem that surfaces in the study of the local library consortium as an institutional form of library collaborative activity is the fact that it is virtually impossible to create a satisfactory definition of a local library network amid the great variety of functions that they exhibit, the types of libraries they include, the variation in tradition and local need, the complexity of their respective missions. This condition is further compounded because the terminology that one customarily uses to describe these entities, such as "library consortium," "library system," "library network," "library cooperative," or "library association," is elusive, vague and unspecific, connotes different meanings in different settings, and is dynamic and currently experiencing voluminous usage. A "consortium" can be an international business or a banking concern, or simply society or association. "Local" can specify the stops in a public transportation conveyance, or it can mean simply serving the needs of a limited district. The terms "network" and "system" have been used so often as to produce several hundred thousand "hits" in Dialindex on Dialog.

MODEL

To circumvent this problem of terminology and to establish a framework for viewing the issues and needs of a local library consortia it is beneficial to formulate a model from social science concepts that are sometimes used in the study of institutions. Organizational development and behavior can be viewed in terms of the concept of "institutions," and this concept is quite harmonious with the organization, workings, and functional activity of library consortia and networks of all varieties.

An institution is usually defined as a combination of group beliefs and group activities, organized into a relatively permanent fashion for the purpose of fulfilling some kind of group need. Mature institutions usually have developed a body of customs and traditions, a code of rules and standards, physical extensions such as buildings and technologies, facilities for communication and indoctrination, and often some kind of punitive devices to insure adherence to group norms.[2] Formal institutions such as the Church, the State, or the University are examples of phenomena that are customarily studied in this model, but the concepts apply with equal validity to less formally organized institutions such as library consortia or networks.

DEFINITION OF A LOCAL LIBRARY CONSORTIUM

Relying on this model, then, one can derive a broad definition of a local library consortium as any combination of more than two libraries sharing roughly similar beliefs and purposes, a set of common library and information activities, organized into a relatively permanent fashion for the purpose of fulfilling a group information need of a limited geographical district. A sustaining characteristic of the local library consortium is proximity, and this favorable distance relationship among its membership is the primary reason for its existence as an organization distinct from other forms of collaboration among library entities. This definition is sufficiently broad enough to include libraries of all types, sizes, and specialty, but it deliberately makes no attempt to set distance limits on the size of the local district served since this is a relative factor and can vary from locale to locale.

Because the relationship of technology to the current local consortium contributes to its tangled identity, because technology is often viewed as an instrument for bridging distances, and because technology has fundamentally altered the activities of local library consortia, the local consortia and networks comprehended in this definition have been arbitrarily limited to local consortia whose members are to some degree organizationally dependent upon computation, telecommunications, and machine readable data in carrying out their functions. This definition may exclude some local consortia, but it will encompass the largest majority of formally organized local library consortia with which I am familiar. The terms "network" and "consortium" are used interchangeably in this paper, in the sense of Atkinson's observation, as "handy" terms for describing a group.[3] It is estimated that the number of local library consortia who meet the criteria established by this definition exceeds 300 and is growing.[4]

NETWORKING CULTURE

It has been suggested here that the local library consortium has a tangled identity in that the local library consortium is firmly entrenched in the whole "culture" of library collaboration and networking, and as such it draws heavily upon this larger culture of networking for the sources of much of its thought about library collaboration, much of its program activity, and much of its technology for carrying out its goals. In fact, the local consortium is systemically intertwined with this larger networking culture, simultaneously deriving benefits from the association while incorporating some of its problems. Because of the commercial behavior and competition that characterizes some of the national institutional forms of networking, a case can be made for describing this culture as the National Networking Industry and analyzing its activities from the point of view of a type of trade association in an x-million-dollar industry. For the present discussion, I have chosen to characterize networking as a culture primarily because the belief system which sustains it originates from the not-for-profit and free-access-to-information tradition of individual libraries. It is appropriate, therefore, to place the local library consortium within the broader context of national network activity in order to highlight its distinguishing characteristics.[5]

The contemporary local library consortium, in my judgment, cannot be fully comprehended unless it is viewed as an institutional form within the broader context of this national culture of networking. To accomplish this, I have chosen to categorize all not-for-profit networking and consortia organizations as belonging to one of five distinctive institutional forms of networking. Some of these organizations may perform overlapping functions and share identical belief systems about networking. Although there are exceptions to this taxonomy, in general I believe that the grouping will suffice as a model of networking activity grouped around distinctive primary institutional forms. The model serves as a guide for determining what distinguishes a local library consortium from state, regional, specialized, or national networks.

FIVE FORMS OF NETWORKING

Given the fact that consortia of all types do exhibit considerable similarity in their belief systems, the programs they undertake, and the technologies that they employ, what is it that distinguishes the various consortia and networks from each other? I am able to identify at least five institutional forms of consortia and network activity that exist and are presently sustained by several distinctive purposes and missions: (1) the Unit Cost Networks (2) Multi-State Regional Auxiliary Enterprise Networks, (3) Authority Sanctioned Networks, (4) Discipline and Type-of-Library Networks, and (5) Local Consortia or Proximity Networks.

1. The Unit Cost Networks

These national networks and consortia, primarily the Bibliographic Utilities, were created and still are fundamentally sustained financially by the need to reduce or stabilize the unit costs of performing some function internal to library processing routines such as cataloging, acquisitions, serials control, or interlibrary loan. They are unique among library collaborative institutions by the factor of their size which permits sufficient critical mass necessary to raise substantial capital resources. This capital in turn permits them to engage in research and development activities on a far larger scale than any other library collaborating entity. They perform a major function for the whole networking culture in that they become in effect the de facto nerve centers, the research and development laboratories, the technological support systems, the bibliographic control centers, and the origin of a great deal of thought about sharing activity and functions.

In addition the pricing policies of the unit-cost networks influence the economics of the whole culture of networking (or industry if you prefer) in that they set a kind of benchmark price for much large scale library collaborative activity. Major price fluctuations in the Unit Cost

Networks have the potential to send a shock wave through the membership dependent upon their services. A tangled element in their identity, mission, and scope stems from the fact that it is at times unclear from their behavior whether they are not-for-profit membership organizations or for-profit commercial high-tech ventures.[6] Local library consortia are heavily intertwined with the Unit Cost Networks by purchasing their services, by their members' associations with Unit-Cost Networks, by their participation in the governance of Unit-Cost Networks, and by their use of the Unit Cost Networks as models of successful network activity worthy of emulation. Major policy changes in the unit-cost networks, such as copyright and ownership of data policies, usually have direct impact on local consortia.

2. Multi-State Regional Auxiliary Enterprise Networks

These networks include primarily the regional networks that broker OCLC services and the library service centers. These networks are distinguished by a wide variety of library auxiliary service enterprises requiring low capital investment or fee based assessment to perform. As a general rule, they are limited in their ability to amass large amounts of capital. They perform a significant amount of training and support for automated library operations, and they serve as an influential force interpreting and mediating the issues of networking to their members. They are important players in determining the policies that regulate the whole networking culture. They produce a supply of trained library resource personnel knowledgeable about the intricate and complex technical aspect of library networking that is ordinarily remote from local institutions. As such they play an important gatekeeper role for working librarians in the field, diffusing information about the broader network culture to the membership. The Multi-State Regional Networks perform a variety of services directly for local library consortia, often tailoring services for specific groups. Some observers argue that the Multi-State Regional Auxiliary Enterprise Networks may disappear from the national network culture because they view them as performing middle-man services that are vulnerable.[7] Although this argument is plausible, it does not take into account the intangible factors in the firmly rooted roles these organizations play in the national network culture. I would not anticipate their demise in the foreseeable future, if at all.

3. The Authority-Sanctioned Networks

These networks may, or may not perform functions similar to the two categories of networks mentioned above, but they share common characteristics among themselves derived from the fact they were created and are sustained by sources of governmental authority such as a State Legislature or State Agency. This authority usually comprehends a certain measure of jurisdiction over all, or many, of the libraries in a given state or district. These associations of libraries are in fact state-sanctioned, often giving some of their program planning a top-down approach. They are often supported by a powerful and compelling economic belief system based on the mandate that the greatest use of the authority's limited resources must be achieved for the greatest number of citizens in the jurisdiction. They have additional advantages that top down planning can bring such as the ability to legislate policy, standards, and procedures, and the authority to coerce acceptance of the standards. They have a source of capital for new projects in their procedures for making requests to the funding authority that has established them.

4. The Discipline and Type-of-Library Networks

These networks are distinguished primarily from the other institutional forms of consortia and network activity by the fact that they are created and often sustained by their relationship to a discipline such as Law, Medicine, or Agriculture or to an institutional form such as a university, public school, or a corporation. They often derive their strength and effectiveness from the importance of the discipline or institution in national, state, or local policy. For example, sources of public funding are routinely made available for medical consortia and agricultural consortia both of whom have strong national public policy commitments as seen by both having national libraries attached to the Executive Branch and in the fact that both are active in support of consortia. The sources of funding for these consortia tend to vary with the degree of priority that is given to the disciplines and institutions by Congress and are subject to fluctuation as public policy changes.

5. Local Consortia or Proximity Networks

These networks primarily come into existence and are sustained by proximity and favorable distance relationships among the members. These local consortia vary considerably in size, in organization, in governance, and in programming activity, but some general characteristics apply to all of them. They as a general rule are not involved in research and development, they are limited in their ability to raise large capital funds, and they tend to have programs that make the greatest use of the favorable conditions that close proximity to their membership brings. They are in most cases the least formally organized of the networks, and they might be generally characterized as voluntary associations of members with very few contractual obligations placed upon their membership. They generally have a lower fee structure than most of the other networks, but they are dependent operationally on a sizeable commitment of voluntary staff support from the membership.

CHARACTERISTIC OF LOCAL CONSORTIA

The distinguishing characteristic of local consortia from the other existing institutional forms of library collaborative organizations is its ability to take maximum advantage of proximity and favorable distance relationships in carrying out its program activity in much the same way that the authority-sanctioned networks maximize the advantages that jurisdiction over a state or district bestow on their program activities. Proximity among the membership of a local consortia affords the flexibility of experimentation with a variety of low-cost delivery systems, the benefit of low cost communication systems with various telecommunications options, the advantage of increased direct contact among the membership, and the advantage of being a kind of "natural information district" with a more or less perceived locus of operations for library collaboration.

The local library consortium, as a general rule, borrows its belief system about resource sharing and cooperation from the broader context of the national networking culture. It appears that the local consortium has made little effort to elaborate a distinctive belief system grounded on the principle that the local consortium is a generic institutional form of library collaboration with certain unique programmatic features. Typically the belief system has been premised upon the principles associated with resource sharing, even though local consortia participate in activities and functions that go well beyond materials resource sharing.

BELIEF SYSTEM

Although the belief system that sustains resource sharing in the networking culture generally has many variations, a number of primary themes recur in library thought that are repeatedly cited as justifications for consortium activity. These justifications are routinely incorporated into the belief system that sustains the local consortium. Many local variations are based on the premise that no single general library of any type or variety can expect to have all the fiscal and other resources required to build collections that will be sufficiently comprehensive to meet ALL the needs of any reasonably diversified multipurpose user community; hence, there is a need to share, in some manner, both intellectual and physical access to those materials not locally available.[8] From this economic premise of the inability of a single institution to collect what it needs, the belief system can be expanded to include any group of libraries of any geographical scope. It becomes possible then to found a local library consortium on the belief that a gap exists between locally available resources and local need and the local library consortium is a mechanism for addressing the problem of the gap. There are many variations of this theme running throughout the networking thought.

In addition to the economic justification for resource sharing which appears to be the major force that sustains the belief system, other beliefs are sometimes argued as justifications for the formation of local consortia. The belief in the desirability, among some librarians, for the creation of a national library network that can be created from the bottom-up through associations of libraries at the "grass-roots" level, rather than top down from the few central sources of authority.[9] The belief also exists that networks and consortia have a democratic responsibility to address the problem of the gap that exists between the information rich and information poor and that consortium arrangements for sharing information is a balance against the inevitable formation of information elites. Finally, the controversial belief, either stated or implied, among some groups of librarians that the act of cooperation is undeniably good whether or not it achieves any concrete objectives for an individual library.

In this regard the belief system that sustains local library consortia and other forms of the networking culture is characterized by a persistent conflict that is imported into the thought and deliberations of the local consortium. This conflict, which may be regarded as one of the perennial concerns in structuring consortium activity is well illustrated in the contrasting thought of two experienced observers of library networking. One network manager has observed that "cooperation is an unnatural act" while another observer of networking has remarked that "librarians are a cooperative breed."[10]

AMBIVALENCE ABOUT COOPERATION

These contrasting views about the act of cooperation suggest that an ambivalence exists among librarians about the purposes of cooperation and that this ambivalence is reflected in the belief systems that exist about cooperation. It should be noted that this conflict is not unique to library networking thought and that the nation's own historic institutional forms, whether they be corporations, judicial institutions, educational institutions, or libraries are conditioned by the culture toward energetic, vital, and vigorous pursuit of their own self-interest. It is not surprising then to find in the library network culture very able advocates of the proposition that libraries and library managers and network and network directors pursue their own interest and the interests of their organizations. As Ron Miller has observed, "library administrators and network administrators tend to act in their own self-interest rather than in the interest of a dimly defined greater good. . . ."[11] Strong advocates of cooperation continue to react to libraries' functional pursuit of their own interests by characterizing elements in this pursuit as posing "psychological barriers to cooperation."[12] This conflict in the belief system about networking, and its many variations, still characterizes networking and consortium activity of all types, and it surfaces from time to time in many of the issues and concerns of local library consortia.

As has been suggested in this paper, local library consortia exist intertwined in a interwoven pattern of institutional forms of national networking activity that has at least five dominant institutional forms. All of the forms influence the whole and each other in program creation, diffusion of technology, and the belief systems that sustain them. It is not uncommon to find all the members of a local consortium holding several memberships in other institutional forms of networking. In light of these characteristics, what then are the issues and needs facing local library consortia in the present highly linked environment of networking?

ISSUES AND CONCERNS

The present issues and concerns go beyond the traditional concerns of the local consortium as a resource sharing organization. Traditional issues and concerns have centered around the local consequences, problems, and conflicts of autonomous institutions undertaking collaborative action; problems associated with the existing pattern of essentially voluntary, informal, and decentralized institutional sharing associated with interlibrary loan; the high per unit costs associated with sharing resources; problems associated with bibliographical access to collective holdings of members; problems associated with physical access; problems associated with providing equal treatment to equals among libraries which vary in size, type, prestige, age, scope of collections, and legal status; the problem of governance of resource-sharing organizations; and the problems of measurement and evaluation of the resource-sharing organizations.

These traditional problems and issues are important, are in many instances unresolved, and remain very much with us. Judging from the number of local library consortia that have emerged in recent years, however, these problems and issues have not retarded the development of interinstitutional library collaboration at the local level, nor does it appear that they will do so in the future. At this stage in their development, local library consortia appear to be vital, energetic, popular and growing institutions, even if their role, scope, and mission as an institutional form of collaboration at the present time seems to be imperfectly understood and constitutes a tangled identity.

Although still grappling with these fundamental issues of cooperation and resource sharing, the local library consortium, even in its presently vigorous state, faces a new array of needs that have emerged in the rapidly changing local environment and the rapidly changing national network culture. These issues and needs can be grouped under six primary categories.

NEW NEEDS

1. Continuing Redefinition of the Role, Scope, and Mission of the Local Consortium

In light of its position, and the position of much of its membership, heavily intertwined with other institutional forms of collaboration in the national network culture, the local library consortium is presently experiencing a need to rethink its mission in terms of local need, local conditions, and local problems that cannot be effectively addressed by other institutional forms of networking.

This process can benefit from particular examination of consortium activities and programs whose effectiveness is heightened by the natural advantage of proximity such as direct access borrowing and document delivery. In the present environment, the process of redefining its role may also benefit by a recognition of the effectiveness that can be gained in programs that utilize the advantages of proximity in combination with technology. Finally, contemporary redefinition of the role and scope of the local consortium needs to underscore the fact that, of all the institutional forms of networking, the local consortium is situated in closest proximity to the end user, a distinct advantage and a source of much of the local consortium's present strength and vitality.

2. The Technological Form of the Local Consortium

An increasingly important issue facing the local consortium is the need to make a decision on the technological form that is most appropriate for carrying out its role, scope, and mission. A number of alternatives exist for the technological form that a consortium will assume. These include an integrated centralized network form, a mixed network form with a decentralized system for local purposes and a centralized database for sharing purposes, a completely distributed network, or a linked network form with distributed processing. New options emerge with possibilities for distributing the local database, distributing processing, and distributing the telecommunications network. The technological form, it is assumed, should follow the functionality of the local consortium and be harmonious with the role, scope, and mission of the organization.

3. Bibliographic Control

The ultimate information competence of the local library consortium is dependent on the degree of inventory control that the consortium can obtain of the information residing in the district. The problem that bibliographic control presents to a local consortium will vary from region to region, but this issue will be an agenda item for many local consortia for quite some time to come.

4. The Issue of Direct Access

Local consortia have a special concern with the issue of direct physical access to collections and services of its members. The direct-access issue centers around a crucial question for the local consortium which is intensified by the condition of proximity. How far is it feasible to extend the collections, services, staff, and equipment of one library to the collective clientele of the entire consortia? This question is answered in a variety of ways by employing a variety of mechanisms and access procedures in local consortia, but the issue of direct reciprocal access for the entire user community of a local consortium is a contentious issue that will be heightened and intensified as linkages are effected that enable users to quickly identify the holdings of all consortium members.

5. Governance and the Issue of Maintaining Equal Treatment to Equals in a Local Consortium

Very few local library consortia, if any, are able to maintain equilibrium between how much a member contributes to a consortium and how much it receives in return. The issue consistently emerges in the deliberations of consortia and probably will remain a constant. In the present networking environment, however, the issue of complete equity and equality is juxtaposed against the argument that the "values of being in a network are not the same for each participant."[13] Under this value consideration, governance and maintenance of equality in the consortium are largely determined by a collective common sense of the membership who tolerate any perceived inequalities in operation out of an implicit faith in the belief system that sustains the collaboration as valuable.

6. Financing the Local Consortium

Finance of the local consortium promises to be a more difficult issue in the future as the costs of operations rise as they become more dependent upon capital intensive technology, rising maintenance costs of telecommunications, and staffing costs associated with support of local consortia activity and programs. It appears that local library consortia are customarily financed by membership dues, fee assessments, grants, and voluntary contribution of staff time to consortium programs. Individual members of a consortium, heavily intertwined as they are in the national networking culture, may have to set functional priorities among their total networking commitments.

CONCLUSION

Finally, it must be observed that the local library consortium, having matured into a distinctive institutional form of networking, is at the same time so interconnected to the total networking culture that virtually all issues and concerns of national networking have local implications. Issues such as copyright and ownership of data have just as much implication for the local consortium as for the regional or state network. Networking has indeed incorporated libraries into the "global village." Nevertheless, the local consortium, tangled as it is, is a generic institutional form of networking with a special legacy. As has been observed, "The reality is that the majority of library collections, services, and access are provided by local, not national, agencies using local, not national, funds and that any extended access to these local collections has come about through professional cooperation and operational necessity.... the extraordinary access to interlibrary information enjoyed in our country rests on local funding, local initiative, and professional cooperation on a virtually unique scale."[14] Thus, the local consortium has a worthy legacy and, in my judgment, an even brighter future.

NOTES

1. James H. Kennedy, "Network Anatomy and Objectives: Comments," in Allen Kent and Thomas J. Galvin, eds. *The Structure and Governance of Library Networks*. (New York: Marcel Dekker, 1979), p. 23.

2. *Encyclopedia of the Social Sciences*. New York: The MacMillan Co., 1932, Volume 7, p. 84. Walton H. Hamilton, the contributor of this entry observes that "about every urge of mankind an institution grows up." See also Louis Schneider's entry in *A Dictionary of the Social Sciences*, edited by Julius Gould and William Kolb. (New York: Free Press, 1964), p. 338.

3. Hugh C. Atkinson, "Atkinson on Networks," *American Libraries*, 18 (June, 1987), p. 432.

4. Allen Kent identified more than 500 networks and consortia in 1979. Not all of these networks and consortia conform to the criteria established in this paper and my estimate of the number of existing, formally organized, local consortia and networks is lower than his, although the number appears to be growing.

5. *Network-Planning Paper*, Network Development and MARC Standards Office, Library of Congress, by Lenore S. Mauryama, "The Library of Congress Network Advisory Committee: Its First Decade," pp. 9-12.

6. Susan K. Martin, *Library-Networks, 1986-87: Libraries in Partnership*. (White Plains: Knowledge Industry Publications, 1986), p. 122.

7. Susan K. Martin, "Networks: Changing Roles," in "Key Issues in the Networking Field Today," Library of Congress, Network Development and Standards Office, *Network-Planning Paper*, No. 12, 1985, p. 45.

8. Herman Fussler, *Research Libraries and Technology*. (Chicago: The University of Chicago Press, 1973), p. 33.

9. JoAn Segal, "A Common Vision: Networking for Networkers and Librarians," in

Network-Planning Paper, Network Development and MARC Standards Office, Library of Congress, No. 13, 1986, p. 15-16.

10. Martin, *Library Networks*. p. 1. and Martin, "Networks: Changing Roles," p. 37.

11. Ronald Miller, "The Impact of Technology on Library Networks and Related Organizations," p. 49 in *Network-Planning Paper* No. 12.

12. Martin, *Library Networks*, p. 90.

13. Atkinson, "On Networking," p. 432 cited above.

14. Barbara Markuson, "Issues in National Library Network Development: An Overview," p. 16.

Multistate Library Networks: A Model for Lay Representation on Library Network Boards

Louella V. Wetherbee

INTRODUCTION

The purpose of this paper is to review the organization of governing boards of selected multistate library networks and to propose a model for lay representation on these boards.

The paper briefly reviews the literature on network governance as it relates to governing bodies. As very little has been written that specifically refers to the ideal organizational structure for network boards, current models used by regional networks for selecting and organizing boards are reviewed. Particular attention is paid to the role of lay trustees. Other models for securing outside legal, financial and planning expertise also are explored.

The term "trustee" when used in this paper means an elected or appointed member of a network governing board or council. The term "lay trustee" means a person from outside the library and information science community serving on a board.

Some comments also will be made concerning the role of outside expertise in network management as the two functions, management and governance, are interrelated and tend to overlap in some instances. Outside expertise is widely used by networks in both management and governance.

The final section of the paper proposes a model for effective lay representation on network governing boards. Some recommendations are made about recruiting and integrating lay trustees onto network boards.

Louella V. Wetherbee holds a BA in Portuguese from the University of Texas and an MLS also from the University of Texas. She has been Executive Director of the AMIGOS Bibliographic Council since 1984, prior to which she was Director of Libraries at George Mason University. Ms. Wetherbee has been active in numerous library associations and organizations.

© 1988 by The Haworth Press, Inc. All rights reserved.

LIBRARY NETWORK GOVERNANCE

Since the mid-1970s, a number of papers have been written that are either partially or fully devoted to network governance. In 1978, a conference on the structure and governance of library networks was held in Pittsburgh.[1] The issue of network governance is a topic of ongoing concern to the Library of Congress Network Advisory Committee, which sponsored a program in 1980 on governance issues for a nationwide library network.[2] As library participation in networks has increased during the past decade, the importance of developing workable, effective network governance models has increased.

Although libraries cooperate for a variety of reasons, this paper is limited to a discussion of large, multistate networks using automation for the delivery of services. It is likely, however, that many of the factors pertinent to effective governance of these organizations are applicable to other types of resource sharing networks at the state or local level.

In a key 1977 paper on network governance, Stevens noted that network governance had not stabilized around a model. He further noted that no theoretical model existed upon which networks could be built.[3] A decade later, Stevens' assertions regarding the lack of a single viable model for effective network governance are still valid.

In recent years networks have proliferated at the state and local level. This growth has been spurred by the development of shared automated library systems for cataloging, circulation, and other functions. The role of library networks since 1977 has broadened and deepened as a result of the maturation of automated library systems. In addition, a variety of economic and political factors continue to make resource sharing attractive. Several different organizational models for library networks are emerging; it is unlikely that a single model can or should be developed for network governance.

Participation in any library network involves trade-offs for the participants. Kent described this phenomenon in terms of loss of autonomy. He states that "the basic objective of networks frequently entails a shift from reliance on 'local holdings' to reliance on 'access' to materials held elsewhere."[4] Obviously, as network members sense a loss of local control, they will move to regain some portion of that control through participation in the governance of the network.

Carlile emphasizes the importance of laying a proper foundation for networks based on three factors: legal structure, membership or constituency, and governance. He defines governance as "the structure and administration of the power relationships among various organizational stakeholders within the shared activity or network."

Carlile clearly distinguishes between governance and management and provides a succinct and thoughtful list of 22 characteristics that ought to be present in a successful governance model.[5] Several of those characteristics are pertinent to the formation of network governing boards. They include:

—Balanced representation of a diverse constituency in the governance, either directly or indirectly
—Communication from the constituency to governance, and accountability from governance to constituency
—Ability to balance centrality of control and direction with the diverse needs of the constituency
—Assurance of financial stability
—Provision of an interface with the private sector, and federal and state governments
—Ability to avoid political obstacles to performance
—Ability to act on behalf of, protect, and shield the membership
—Ability to provide a united face on behalf of the network to third parties

Although Carlile does not specifically discuss appropriate network board composition, his list of attributes should be kept in mind in the formation and operation of a successful network board.

A key component in network success is the selection, organization and operation of an effective governing board or council. Narrowness in board composition may hamper network development. Along with fair representation of all types and sizes of member libraries, the use of lay representatives on network boards can help insure broad based, non-parochial decision making.

Most networks form a governing board or advisory council which controls policy for the network and makes the relevant decisions concerning scope of service and selection of staff. In some instances, the role of the network board is ambiguous. It may serve primarily an advisory function, but hold some decision making power. This is often the case where the network functions under the aegis of a parent body.

ROLES AND RESPONSIBILITIES OF NETWORK BOARDS

Duca lists the following general categories of board responsibilities in nonprofit organizations:

- Clarify the organization's mission
- Interpret the mission statement to the public and enhance the organization's public image
- Approve goals and objectives/set long-range plans
- Establish policies and other guidelines
- Assume legal responsibility for all aspects of the organization's operations
- Ensure financial stability and solvency
- Hire and support the executive director and assess his performance
- Evaluate the performance of the organization and the board itself[6]

Network boards, especially governing boards of independent member controlled networks, have many or all of these responsibilities. Indeed, the trend among multistate networks such as NELINET, SOLINET and AMIGOS has been toward increased member control through directly elected boards.

Numerous considerations come to mind when developing the optimum board structure: size, composition, organization, and lay representation are among the most common. But just as there can be no single model for overall network governance, there exists no universal model for a network board. If a generalization can be made, it is that the sometimes ambiguous and often conflicting goals of all networks make it imperative for each to assemble a board composed of knowledgeable, objective and involved trustees. A board member who is unable to spend the time necessary to master the key political, economic, and technological issues in the field—or attend board functions—is unlikely to make a meaningful contribution.

Duca divides boards into large (30+ members), medium (20-30 members), and small (fewer than 20 members).[7] All but two of the 12 multistate networks contacted for this paper have boards of 15 or fewer members.

Although most network boards would be classified as small, seven of the 12 boards surveyed for this study currently include elected or appointed voting lay representatives. At least one other network has had lay representatives in the past and is considering a change of bylaws that would mandate lay representation. Of the networks with lay representatives, one is considering dropping lay representation. Where lay representation is not mandated by network governing documents, there are a variety of methods used to secure outside expertise when needed. These alternatives will be discussed later.

The literature on network board composition and organization is quite limited. Network boards, however, can be presumed to share some common factors with library boards since both organizations are in existence for the same ultimate purpose: to provide information services to library patrons. Virginia Young in her book on library trustees notes that:

> . . . every segment of today's society has a stake in the community library, and the needs and desires of every segment of society should be represented in the library's program.[8]

She later writes that library trustees may be called upon to serve on network boards and adds that:

> . . . this demands mastering legal responsibilities of broader scope, handling more money, and somehow raising [the trustee's] library sights above the familiar provincialism of his local library horizons.[9]

In 1971, Hacker cited as a problem in network planning the "possibility that network planners may overlook their responsibilities to the public." His solution:

> Encourage active participation in the evaluation of networks by students, faculty, research personnel, and the general public through advisory committees, *lay network boards of trustees*, and valuation of network performance at regular intervals.[10] (emphasis added)

Pointing up the need for broad representation in network governance structures, Mathews wrote in 1978 that:

> . . . a library network must draw on very diverse talents for input into its governance process. It must not . . . be dominated by a luff of librarians, a mumble of moneymongers, a puff of politicians, a nettle of network directors, or a usurpation of users. . . . There should also be a mix of types and philosophical lean-

ings among the governors—thinkers and doers, speculators and practitioners. . . ."[11]

In a 1974 report on the feasibility of a cooperative bibliographic center for Indiana, Markuson comments:

> The INCOLSA Executive Director and Executive Committee should avail themselves of outside expertise in management. For example, there is free expertise available on a short-time basis from experienced retired and active business executives through SCORE (Service Corps of Retired Executives) and ACE (Active Corps of Executives) for which INCOLSA may be eligible.[12]

Given that network boards tend to be small, it is important to consider the role of each member of the board. Network boards are elected by network members and have a responsibility to represent the interests of their constituents. If lay trustees are to be used, their selection and integration into network affairs needs to be carefully planned.

Among networks that have chosen to use lay trustees, a variety of models for their selection and participation have evolved. Both these models and other methods for securing outside financial, legal and planning expertise are reviewed below. As noted above, some networks have a second governance body above the member-elected board. For example, the CAPCON Board of Advisors reports to a parent board. Only the board or council closest to the network membership is fully explored here.

NETWORK BOARD COMPOSITION

(The majority of the information contained in this section was collected through interviews which the author conducted with the directors or other representatives of the networks included in this paper. Other sources are appropriately noted.)

AMIGOS (AMIGOS Bibliographic Council, Inc.)

AMIGOS is a nonprofit regional network serving the southwestern U.S. and Mexico. The AMIGOS Board is composed of twelve trustees directly elected by the network members. The trustees serve three-year, overlapping terms. Nine trustees are selected from among registered representatives of member institutions and three must be persons who are or have been active in civic, private or institutional management. Persons who may be considered include academic officials, state or local governmental officials, private corporation executives and community leaders. One of the three lay trustees should have had demonstrated experience and competence in fiscal affairs.[13] AMIGOS has had lay trustees from all of the above categories, including a data processing manager for a large city, a university dean, a university vice-president for fiscal affairs, a microcomputer company president, a financial management consultant, and an attorney. The lay trustees are nominated in the same manner as library member trustees. Although they normally have not been elected to a principal office, they are frequently on committees.

BCR (Bibliographic Center for Research)

BCR, a nonprofit organization serving libraries in the Rocky Mountain states, has existed since the 1930s. It currently is governed by a 13-member Board of Trustees with mixed membership; seats are mandated in the bylaws for the chief officer of each state library member (five at present). In addition there are five representative trustees and three at-large trustees. The representative trustees are elected according to type of library.[14] A recent reorganization of the board resulted in extending the vote to all trustees. Formerly, only the state library trustees were able to vote, while the other seats were advisory and nonvoting. BCR has not used lay trustees, although outside legal and financial expertise is used, both pro-bono and paid.

CAPCON (Capital Consortium Network)

CAPCON is a program of the Consortium of Universities of the Metropolitan Washington Area, a nonprofit corporation. CAPCON serves libraries in the District of Columbia, Maryland and Virginia. The CAPCON Board of Advisors acts as an advisory body to the Consortium, but has had specific responsibilities delegated to it, including setting fees and determining criteria for network membership and participation. The Consortium retains final authority over selection of an Executive Director. The Board of Advisors is composed of nine elected members, seven of whom are the chief administrative officers of member libraries and two of whom are "nonlibrarians or non-practicing librarians active in business, civic, or political areas."[15] A new structure is currently under consideration which would result in the elimination of the requirement for non-library trustees. This same proposal also would mandate representation on the Board by type and size of library.[16] Lay Trustees in the past have included retired librarians and an attorney. The network seeks outside expertise in the legal and financial areas. In the latter area, lay trustees of the parent board are able to provide advice, while legal assistance is hired as needed.

CLASS (Cooperative Library Agency for Systems and Services)

Organized under a "Joint Exercise of Powers Agreement" among various California jurisdictions, CLASS serves libraries nationwide, although the majority of members are in the west. Six voting seats on the Board of Directors are allocated to the original parties to the agreement. The Board was enlarged in 1981 to include nine nonvoting members who are elected on a proportional basis from among the various segments of the membership: academic libraries, community college/school libraries, state libraries, public libraries, and special/other libraries. As a consequence of the governance model chosen, CLASS has a number of lay trustees. The six voting members are the chief officers or their designees from the original parties to the agreement, including the California State Librarian, the President of the University of California, the Chancellors of the state university and community college systems, the Mayor of Los Angeles, and a member of the Santa Clara County Board of Supervisors.[17] In addition, nonvoting members may be nonlibrarians. In the past, a lay representative has been elected to represent the special library membership segment.

FEDLINK (Federal Library and Information Network)

FEDLINK derives its authority from the Federal Library and Information Committee (FLICC). It has an Executive Advisory Council consisting of nine members serving staggered terms. Although not a governing body in the strict sense of the word, the EAC exercises considerable power. The EAC has responsibility for setting policy, establishing and charging committees, recommending budgets to the membership, overseeing the annual budget, authorizing contracts, and settling disputes concerning membership or voting.[18]

There are no mandated seats on the board, but informal consideration is given to securing representation from the three branches of government. No lay persons are on the EAC. Outside assistance, when needed, is either contracted for or provided by the Library of Congress.

MINITEX (Minnesota Interlibrary Telecommunications Exchange)

MINITEX functions under the aegis of the Higher Education Coordinating Board of the state of Minnesota (HECB). The network is a program of the HECB. It serves libraries in Minnesota, North Dakota, and South Dakota. A MINITEX Advisory Committee exists to "advise [the HECB] regarding policies, programs, goals and planning."[19] The Advisory Committee, appointed by the HECB, is composed of thirteen members who are elected from various library constituencies. There is no elected lay council member, but the HECB program officer responsible for MINITEX, a non-librarian, serves in an ex-officio capacity on the council. In addition, HECB is also advised by a MINITEX/OCLC Users Group composed of OCLC participating libraries. Both bodies serve an advisory role only and do not include elected lay members. Assistance in financial and/or legal areas comes through the HECB staff. Long range planning has been accomplished by network members.

NELINET, Inc.

NELINET is organized as a nonprofit network. Although not limited by its bylaws in geographic scope, NELINET operates chiefly in the New England states, with headquarters in Massachusetts. The Board of Directors can be composed of from three to fifteen members, elected by the members, and who serve three-year overlapping terms. Normally twelve members are elected. The NELINET Executive Director is a voting Board member.[20]

There are no mandated seats based on geography, type or size of library, nor is there provision for lay membership on the Board of Directors. Consideration has been given in the past to such representation, but when outside expertise is required, it usually is hired. NELINET has included a nonvoting member on the Board Finance Committee on two occasions. These individuals served without compensation. One was a comptroller in an academic institution and the other was a business school professor. Other external assistance has included hiring legal expertise and retaining a consulting firm for development of a long range plan.

OCLC (OCLC Online Computer Library Center, Inc.)

OCLC is organized as a nonprofit corporation in the state of Ohio. It has grown from a state network to an international organization, and its governance structure has undergone changes appropriate to a growing organization. This rather complex structure is described in detail in the literature.[21] The OCLC Board of Trustees is comprised of fifteen voting members selected in several different ways to insure broad representation of interests. Frederick Kilgour, the founder of OCLC, serves as the sixteenth nonvoting board member. Of the voting members, five must be from:

> ... categories such as ... an executive officer of a large corporation; an individual experienced in banking and finance; an individual with background or present service in government, national, state or local; an economist; an accountant with experience in taxation and business enterprise; an attorney with experience in corporation law; an individual with experience in electronic computer science or industry; an individual with experience in communications technology; an individual with marketing and distribution knowledge....[22]

Three trustees must be members of the library profession and six are elected by the OCLC Users Council from among its own membership.

PALINET and Union Library Catalog of Pennsylvania

PALINET is a nonprofit corporation providing library services principally to libraries in the middle Atlantic states, although the network may operate wherever the Board of Trustees directs. The Board is composed of fifteen voting members serving staggered terms. Thirteen trustees are elected by the members and "two shall be appointed by the Board from the public-at-large."[23] The appointed lay trustees have usually been drawn from the legal or banking professions. The Board often selects from among candidates identified by the network director. The lay trustees do not usually serve on committees, but the Finance Committee does include a banker. Additional outside expertise in the areas of finance, legal matters or strategic planning has been hired as needed.

PRLC (Pittsburgh Regional Library Center)

PRLC is organized as a nonprofit corporation in the state of Pennsylvania devoted to the promotion of various services to libraries in Pittsburgh and surrounding areas. Each library member annually designates two persons to serve as trustees of the Center. One of the two trustees appointed by each member is the head librarian or another senior library staff member.[24]

When PRLC was formed, there were only nine network members, and this structure was quite workable. Given the growth of the network, a committee has been formed to consider reorganization of the governance structure. According to the network director, the original intent was to have each institution appoint a librarian and a non-librarian trustee; currently approximately ten percent of the trustees are lay people. Lay trustees have included library trustees, academicians, and computer center personnel. Most lay trustees have not been particularly active members, although some have.

Additional outside expertise also is used. PRLC has retained a financial planner for investment decisions. Legal advice is provided at a preferential rate through the firm of an attorney serving on the board. No outside assistance for planning has been used recently.

SOLINET (Southeastern Library Network, Inc.)

SOLINET operates as a tax exempt organization whose primary service area includes the southeastern United States. By board action, SOLINET may operate in the Caribbean basin and in portions of Central and South America. The Board of Directors has eleven members who serve three-year overlapping terms. Five of the seats are allocated to representatives of the Association of Southeastern Research Libraries (ASERL). Four are elected from among representatives of other academic libraries and the remaining two are from non-academic member libraries. Although no seats are required to be filled by lay trustees, the bylaws provide that "directors shall be affiliated with a member institution as an administrator, professional employee, or representative of the governing board of the institution."

SOLINET is currently considering enlarging the board to thirteen members. One of the thirteen members would be elected by the other directors. This person would be a senior administrator from a college, a university or local government.

SOLINET has utilized outside expertise in several ways. University and community college administrators have served on previous boards. The Board Financial Advisory Committee has a lay financial advisor. Although not a board member, this individual is invited to board meetings. SOLINET has worked with the Executive Service Corps of United Way, and the network has been assigned, at its request, a team of retired executives who advise management on personnel and financial matters as well as strategic planning. At other times, the SOLINET Board has sought technical expertise through a Technical Advisory Committee composed of computer experts. SOLINET retains a local firm for legal advice, but in the past has had a staff attorney.

WLN (Western Library Network)

WLN operates under the auspices of the Washington State Library Commission and serves libraries principally in the Pacific northwest. A Network Services Council recommends policy on network services to the Commission. The Council has a major role in reviewing long range plans, budgets and network fees, but does not control these directly.

The Council is made up of not more than eleven members. Four members of the Council are selected from Washington state, of whom three must be principal members who own or lease terminals. Representatives from other states are elected as each state determines. One member serves from each of the other states where at least three libraries participate in the network computer service.[25] Although the Council bylaws would not seem to prohibit the election of a lay person, normally the council members are librarians.

WLN does not seem to make extensive use of outside expertise in the areas of finance, legal issues, or long range planning. The state treasurer's office and the state attorney general provide help in the first categories and planning is done in-house with input from the Network Services Council. Although the Council does not include lay persons, the parent state commission is composed largely of non-librarians, including an attorney, a financial consultant, a retired economics professor, and the state superintendent of public instruction.

OUTSIDE EXPERTISE: THE OPTIONS

This review of network practices indicates that networks commonly use outside expertise in decision making. The major areas where assistance has been sought include financial management, investments, budget preparation, legal issues, technical planning, long range or strategic planning, network organization, and personnel matters.

A wide range of methods for securing competent outside expertise is observed, with many networks using more than one method, including:

— Elected lay trustees
— Appointed lay trustees
— Advisors to board committees
— Advisory committees to the board composed of outside experts
— Pro-bono legal and financial advice from persons unaffiliated with the network members
— Pro-bono advice from employees of member organizations
— Pro-bono advice from trustees or staff of parent organizations
— Reduced rate legal advice
— Volunteer experts (usually retired executives) as advisors to management and/or board

Five of the larger networks with self-governing boards including OCLC, SOLINET, AMIGOS, PALINET and CLASS have a tradition of lay membership on their respective boards; networks with advisory bodies seem less likely to have lay representatives on the advisory group, relying on parent organizations for needed expertise in specialized areas. The networks that have traditionally used elected or appointed lay trustees have similar requirements for the types of individuals who should be selected. A review of these characteristics will shed light on the kinds of expertise that networks must have available to function effectively.

Networks should consider the implications of these skills for future network staff development. OCLC and, to some extent, SOLINET and AMIGOS have moved toward integration of employees with training in specialized areas. OCLC has in-house legal, financial and strategic planning officers. AMIGOS and SOLINET each have in-house financial officers and SOLINET has had a staff attorney.

Elected or appointed lay network trustees seem to have similar characteristics. AMIGOS has divided the desired skills and experience of lay trustees into three categories. These categories are suggested along with a fourth category to accommodate nonmanagement expertise. The categories are listed here with examples of generic titles of actual trustees who have served on different network boards:

Category A: Civic Management
    — National, state, or local elected government officials such as mayors, or county supervisors

—State or local government employees
Category B: Private Management
—Attorneys
—Bankers
—Corporation or company presidents/chief executive officers
—Corporate legal counsel
—Corporate financial officers
—Corporate data processing managers
—Corporate marketing specialists
—Corporate computer/communications officers
—Financial managers
—Financial management consultants
Category C:
—University/college presidents/deans
—University system administrators
—Academic fiscal affairs officers
—Community college administrators
Category D: Non-Managerial Expertise
—Library trustees
—Professors

The presence of government employees or elected officials on network boards provides some insurance that the network will take into account the needs of the larger community in planning. A link to decision makers in community and state government is essential for sound network planning. Although this can be accomplished informally by the network manager, trustees from this category can strengthen the tie.

Representatives of private management frequently are asked to serve on network boards. Their contribution appears to center primarily on providing financial and legal advice. They also advise on network planning needs, computer and telecommunications technology issues and act as informal "management consultants" to network trustees and staff.

At least three networks in this study mentioned the use of retired company executives as either board members or other types of network advisors. This avenue of readily available, low-cost expertise could be tapped by networks who need outside management advice but have no provision for lay trustees.

The frequent mention of financial and legal expertise as desirable background for lay trustees indicates that networks may have increasingly complex needs in these areas. As budgets grow and service areas expand, networks find that a bookkeeper is no longer enough to manage network financial affairs. Networks will continue to move toward hiring in-house expertise in these areas; these resources can then be supplemented with advice from lay trustees.

Networks have a history that links them closely to the academic library community. A number of networks began as programs that grew out of higher education consortia; several others mentioned above, notably MINITEX and CAPCON, have retained their identity as programs within an academic body. SOLINET clearly demonstrates this close link by providing for dedicated seats on its board for ASERL libraries. It is easy to understand the common presence on network boards of academicians. However, as networks expand beyond the university/college environment, as have all the networks in this paper, new implications for appropriate representation on boards begin to arise. SOLINET, for example, is reviewing a proposed board enlargement to provide a guaranteed seat for a public library representative. It may soon become more common to see city and or county administrators join their counterparts from the academic community on network boards.

This change will surely occur over a period of time, but the history of networking will continue to guarantee a strong voice to the academic community in terms of both practitioners and lay trustees. The costs of participation in many networks which have technologically powerful and expensive programs as their main thrust will slow the integration of other library constituencies into networking. This is the case with both public and school libraries.

Library trustees have served on network boards, but they did not emerge as a major group. Additional links between library boards and network boards undoubtedly would be beneficial for networking. The library end-user might thus have a larger voice in key network decisions.

A MODEL FOR LAY REPRESENTATION

Networks very clearly need and want outside expertise in several areas. They have evolved a variety of innovative ways of securing that assistance. While no one model is always appropriate, the use of lay trustees has some important advantages and constitutes an efficient and effective model.

Consistency

If written into the bylaws of the network, lay trusteeship can become a normal part of network governance. Over a period of time, this will build a corps of informed and committed lay trustee alumni who can return to their posts with a greater understanding of the importance of networks in the provision of quality library and information service to their communities. This benefit is long-term and is of great potential importance as libraries and the networks that serve them compete for scarce public resources.

Commitment

Members of the public-at-large, when elected or appointed to a network board, will have a deeper commitment to the network than if asked simply to provide advice on an ad hoc basis. As a network board member, the trustee can become part of the network environment. Although networks have effectively used lay persons as advisors, board membership provides a broader opportunity to utilize the full range of talents of the volunteer.

While network trustees can serve effectively in appointed positions, trustees who stand for election must think about the responsibility of board membership. In the case of AMIGOS, lay nominees to the board are asked to prepare a brief position statement that is distributed to voting members. In addition, lay trustee nominees attend the network election and are expected to speak to the members about their viewpoints. Such advance preparation encourages an early commitment to the organization by the potential trustees.

Objectivity

There are some inherent potential conflict of interest issues for network member trustees. Lay trustees can act as objective voices on the board. For example, trustees are frequently faced with decisions that cause them to put network interests (the welfare of all members) above local interests (welfare of a single library). This could occur when a proposed fee change might benefit the majority of members but raise costs for a small group of libraries. Lay trustees are less likely to be affected by such conflicts.

End-User Representation

Lay trustees can provide a voice in network decision making for the end-user. Networks are far removed from the actual service delivery that they support through libraries. It is useful to keep the needs of the end-user in mind as network programs are planned. Lay trustees from the public-at-large can fill this role.

Critical Skills

An obvious reason for the addition of lay trustees to network boards is their expertise. This reason for including the lay person with special skills will diminish as networks increasingly seek outside advice in the legal, financial, and planning areas on a fee basis and integrate staff members with special training. Still, the value of board members with broad business, civic or institutional experience should not be underestimated. Networks are arcane organizations, whose role and function is difficult to explain to the general public. There are long-term benefits for networks that cultivate board members from among the informed decision makers and policy makers in their communities, particularly where such individuals can offer concrete advice to the network in setting goals, designing, and funding programs.

Once a decision has been made to integrate lay trustees into network governing bodies, the existing board and network management must take an active role to insure the successful participation of these individuals. The key factors are these:

Identifying Appropriate Candidates

Network boards, staff and members all can provide assistance. A broad pool of potential trustees should be sought. Network staff should continually be alert to identify possible lay trustees.

Interviewing Potential Board Members

The network manager and the board president should conduct a preliminary interview with potential board members. The requirements of board membership should be spelled out in detail including time commitment, preparation, travel, etc. The interview should include an overview of network goals and plans, the financial basis for the network, and a description of the protection offered to trustees in terms of indemnification and directors' and officers' insurance.

Providing Network Orientation

Once a lay trustee has been elected or appointed to the board, a full orientation to network activities should take place prior to the first board meeting. One network director noted that lay trustees receive the same three hour orientation as network member trustees. He felt it was adequate, but found that library and network jargon was an impediment. Another director commented that all trustees need an orientation to network issues while lay trustees might also need orientation to library issues.

Orientation methods vary from network to network. For example, SOLINET, AMIGOS and PALINET hold formal orientation sessions that include all trustees. SOLINET holds a day-long meeting at which old and new board members meet together; formal presentations are made by the board chairperson and network staff. New trustees receive a board manual. Informal orientation is supplied to lay members by several networks.

Recognizing Service

When trustees complete their terms, their home organizations should receive a letter of appreciation for their service. This applies equally to lay trustees and to library trustees. Such a step helps recognize the contribution made by the trustee and raises the image of the network.

In summary, networks need access to a wide range of expertise to function effectively. No single network manager or board member can supply this expertise. Networks should utilize multiple methods for securing advice. An excellent method that should receive particular attention is the inclusion of lay trustees on network boards.

NOTES

1. Allen Kent and Thomas J. Galvin, eds., *The Structure and Governance of Library Networks: Proceedings of the 1978 Conference in Pittsburgh, Pennsylvania.* New York: Marcel Dekker, 1979.

2. *A Nationwide Network: Development, Governance, Support; Discussion Paper . . . from a Meeting Held by the . . . Network Advisory Committee, October 1-2, 1980.* Washington, DC: Library of Congress, 1981.

3. Charles H. Stevens. "Governance of Library Networks," *Library Trends*, (Fall, 1977), p. 219.

4. Allen Kent, "Network Anatomy and Network Objectives," in *The Structure and Governance of Library Networks*, ed. by Allen Kent and Thomas J. Galvin. New York: Marcel Dekker, 1979, p. 4.

5. Huntington Carlile, "The Diversity of Legal Structures Among Networks," in *Net-*

works for Networkers, Barbara Evans Markuson and Blanche Woolls, eds. New York: Neal-Schuman, 1980, pp. 191-193.

6. Diane J. Duca, *Nonprofit Boards: A Practical Guide to Roles, Responsibilities, and Performance*. Phoenix: Oryx Press, 1986, p. 23.

7. *Ibid.*, p. 16.

8. Virginia C. Young. *The Library Trustee: A Practical Guidebook*. New York: R. R. Bowker, 1969, p. 16.

9. *Ibid.*, p. 116.

10. Harold S. Hacker, "Implementing Network Plans: Jurisdictional Considerations in the Design of Library Networks," in *Proceedings of the Conference on Interlibrary Communications and Information Networks . . . Held . . . September 20, 1970-October 2, 1970*, Joseph Becker, ed. Chicago: American Library Association, 1971, p. 245.

11. William D. Mathews, "The Impact of Technology on the Governance of Library Networks," in *Structure and Governance of Library Networks*. New York: Marcel Dekker, 1979, p. 133.

12. Barbara Markuson, "The Indiana Cooperative Library Services Authority—A Plan for the Future." Indianapolis: Indiana State Library, 1974, p. 117.

13. AMIGOS Bibliographic Council, Inc., "Bylaws," Sec. VI.

14. Bibliographic Center for Research, Rocky Mountain Region, Inc., "Restated Bylaws, as adopted . . . February 23, 1983," Art. II.

15. Capital Consortium Network (CAPCON), "Rules and Regulations," Art. IV.

16. *CAPCON Newsletter*, Winter, 1987, p. 6.

17. Cooperative Library Agency for Systems and Services (CLASS) "Bylaws," Art. IV.

18. Federal Library and Information Network (FEDLINK), "Bylaws," August 16, 1984, Art. IV.

19. MINITEX/OCLC Users Group, "A Statement Regarding Its Roles, Responsibilities and Relationships," (undated), p. 1.

20. NELINET, Inc., "Bylaws," Art. III.

21. *A New Governance Structure for OCLC: Principles and Recommendations*. Cambridge, MA: Arthur D. Little, 1977.

22. OCLC Online Computer Library Center, Inc., "Code of Regulations," Art. VII.

23. PALINET and Union Library Catalogue of Pennsylvania, "Bylaws," Art. IV.

24. Pittsburgh Regional Library Center, "Bylaws, rev. May 15, 1986," Art. VI.

25. Western Library Network, Network Services Council, "Bylaws, September 1986," Sec. 2.

Vision and Reality: The Research Libraries and Networking

Paul M. Gherman

THE ROLE OF RESEARCH LIBRARIES

Our profession moves forward first by its leaders having a vision of what can be, then by the testing and striving to create that vision, and finally by several steps backwards as reality adjusts what was foreseen. Always though the target is before us, and our ultimate achievement is that goal. From the beginning of the networking movement in this country, research librarians have had an important role to play. Because of their size, the resources to be brought to bear, and the expected research orientation of the librarians, research libraries have been prime movers in advancing the profession toward networking and resource sharing. Although their holdings are the richest and most varied, so are their demands most varied and immediate. The confluence of technology and the recognition by research libraries that no one library can hope to own the resources needed for modern research have been the genuses of networking.

Although they may not hold as many leadership positions in today's network organizations, research library directors still do exert significant influence on the future of networking in this country. Their goals and agendas will be important forces in shaping the future of resource sharing efforts. Understanding their personal attitudes and agendas as they relate to the current networking objectives, and to technological change, can help in planning for the future. In the winter of 1986-87 the author asked the U.S. membership of the Association of Research

---

Paul M. Gherman has a BA in English and History from Wayne State University and a MALS from the University of Michigan. He is currently the Director of Libraries at Virginia Tech, Blacksburg, VA 24061. He is a member of American Library Association, Association of College and Research Libraries, Virginia Library Association, and the Virginia Center for the Book.

Libraries to comment on the Library of Congress' Network Advisory Committee statement on networking and on the impact of the new technology on their attitudes towards networks. To varying degrees, thirty-eight directors responded either by mail or phone. Their comments were wide-ranging and not consistent; however, certain recurring comments concerning multitype networks, the role of regional networks and OCLC, and their agenda for developing local systems helped to clarify the author's thinking about specific network issues we face today.

The Network Advisory Statement, the text of which was sent to the ARL directors, is ambitious and egalitarian in its stance. It calls for a network environment in which each individual will have "equal opportunity for access to information needs and interests. All users should have access on a timely basis to the information they require without being faced with costs beyond their own or society's means."[1] Also in their statement, NAC recognizes that the dream of a single monolithic network is no longer a possibility. Instead they envision a "coordinated structure of networks."

MULTITYPE NETWORKS

Susan K. Martin, in her study of research library directors' reaction to network governance, foresaw that "as economic and political conditions change, 'motherhood and apple pie' will probably decreasingly reflect reality and institutional goals."[2]

Based on the reaction to the first part of the NAC statement her assumptions are probably correct. Directors of research libraries first and foremost must serve their primary clientele; the immediate academic community, and within that community the researcher and scholar. Research libraries by their very nature and mission are elitist and far from egalitarian. At the same time there is the increasing recognition that information has value, is a commodity, and that there are specific and inherent costs in all aspects of its storage, access and delivery. The more that vendors sell information and not books, the more research librarians realize that they are part of an economic system as well as an information system. As this realization takes hold, networking becomes more an economic decision than one of "apple pie and motherhood." Accordingly, the goal of "the greatest good for the greatest number" is tempered by the recognition that nothing is free, by the desire to avoid exploitative imbalance of services between libraries, and by a preference for contractual or cost-based transactions over open-ended moral commitment.

Barbara Robinson draws an insightful analogy between the dynamics at work in a network and an invitation to a dinner party.[3] There is an understanding that for something offered, the invitation and a meal, a timely reciprocal invitation of equal value will be received in exchange. Likewise, in non-monetary exchanges, there is an underlying understanding that the exchange will be between equals. Rarely does someone of markedly differing economic class invite someone of another economic level to a dinner party with an understanding of reciprocity. With this analogy in mind, it is not at all surprising to find that research librarians have reservations about joining in multitype networks that are based on reciprocity and are not clearly contractual. OCLC's success in attracting a wide variety of types and sizes of libraries, and in retaining the loyalty of many research libraries, may be based to a great extent on the perception that each library has a contract with OCLC and not with the group as a whole. Research libraries feel protected by the contractual arrangement from the fear of reciprocity inherent in many multitype networks with a membership of varying size and resources. Within OCLC, the research library's primary commitment is to the cataloging system which has as its key goal the creation of a national database. The exodus of research libraries from OCLC to RLG was to a utility that stressed a partnership of equals with common needs and goals that range beyond the single goal of a national database.

Most research libraries are, of course, members of state multitype networks that have a wide range of membership from the smallest public library to the flagship academics. In most of these state multitype networks, the research libraries and the major public libraries are the net lenders. It would appear that there would be little benefit to the research library in maintaining membership except that state networks are political. Research libraries must maintain active membership in the state networks because the legislatures perceive state-supported research libraries to be a state resource to be shared with other constituencies. Fear of loss of funding and goodwill prompts research libraries to remain in the state networks. Such intangible sources of motivation, taken together with the unequal distribution of sacrifice within most state networks, may suggest doubt about their long-term viability.

Many research library directors commented on the fact that their current most important agenda was the implementation of a local system. The choice of an automated system is a major local decision whose significance typically pushes aside concerns about resource sharing. As research libraries make this choice, rarely is state network compatibility high on the list of factors driving the decision. The belief that the Linked Systems Project or OSI will someday draw all disparate systems together may also give directors greater license to make local system decisions based on local priorities. Yet it is compatibility that can be a strong factor in the success of a state multitype network. States such as Florida and Illinois have each made a conscious decision to develop a network based on a local system from a single vendor, and more recently, the major state supported academic libraries in Michigan have chosen NOTIS as their local system. The network in Illinois can stand for a model of success: not only do they have local system compatibility, but they have modified the interlibrary loan code to the advantage of the research libraries. Libraries in the network may borrow books from another library in the system in lieu of recalling the book from their own patron. In this system, the University of Illinois, the largest state supported library in the country, is a net borrower.[4] If similar interlibrary loan codes and compatible local systems displaying circulation status could be established in other states, the research libraries might lend their full support to multitype networks.

It is interesting to note that in Florida and Michigan NOTIS has been the local system of choice. Wayne State University and the Detroit Public Library have joined together in the use of a single NOTIS system. Subsequently a number of other smaller local libraries have joined with them to form a multitype network. In the last two years, a number of research libraries have selected NOTIS as their local system. (Twenty-one academic in 1986 alone.)[5] One can imagine that one day a critical mass of research libraries using NOTIS could be reached. NOTIS would then become the de facto local system of research libraries, leading the way to a linked system for research libraries. In this country central planning for such a network could never take place; however, in the current environment each local decision does tend to impact the larger network agenda, and those decisions made at the research library level seem to have greater effect. Were such a system to develop, there would be either the need for smaller libraries to accept a partnership with the research libraries using NOTIS or forego direct access to the research libraries.

THE LOCAL SYSTEM—THE NATIONAL AGENDA

One of the key agendas of research librarians today is the development of local systems and their delivery to the local communities of scholars. In the late 1970s and early 1980s, research libraries were devoting their time to the integration of OCLC or RLG into their technical service and interlibrary loan activities. At the same time they were introducing automated literature searching into the reference process. Microcomputers and their use in auxiliary functions were also proliferating as the staff attained a much higher level of computer literacy. Now turn-key local systems are being installed at a rapid pace, so that soon OPACS and circulation, acquisitions, and serial check-in systems will be a reality in most large academic libraries.

At the same time several larger universities are installing multimillion dollar telecommunications networks on their campuses. These new local networks will have the potential of connecting thousands of end-users and their intelligent terminals to the library. Delivery of library services across these networks will command the research librarians attention well into the 1990s. Indeed, this task may become so all-consuming and may so dramatically change the very nature of the research library that our current concepts of networking may become obsolete. Library services delivered over the local network will likely consist of more than access to the OPAC. The new optical storage media will make tremendous amounts of data accessible in electronic format at local sites without the use of costly telecommunications and, therefore, without the need for networks as we know them today. New relationships may well develop between the publishers of scholarly works, the bibliographic utilities, and research libraries, as the scholar has a more immediate link to information and the structure of scholarly communication changes. Presumably RLG's recognition of the importance of this trend explains its keen interest in the "scholar's workstation."

Several research library directors expressed a growing skepticism over the need for regional networks that serve as links to OCLC. In the initial stages of implementing automation and OCLC, research libraries needed the regionals for staff training and advice. Now that OCLC is fully implemented in research libraries, and now that staff in these libraries have attained a much higher level of sophistication in automation, there is the perception that the regionals are using the funding generated by research libraries to support training in smaller libraries which have only recently joined OCLC. Some of the regional networks have diversified and developed alternative products and services in addition to OCLC brokering, although it is doubtful that these products and services would be sufficiently lucrative to offset the revenue loss created by the departure of research library members. Research libraries do have an abiding commitment to providing as extensive a bibliographic database as possible. It is likely, therefore, that they will not withdraw fully from the use of OCLC.

Optical storage media offer research libraries cost saving alternatives to OCLC. A library could easily subscribe to the LC laser disk of MARC records and download these records to its local system, thus avoiding using OCLC. The savings of OCLC ftu charges and reduction in the number of terminals needed could save the medium sized ARL library approximately $30,000 per year. Since the cost per record use would be eliminated, a larger library could save even more. Original cataloging and holdings could be tape-loaded to OCLC to support the continued integrity of the national database with a potential decrease in timeliness, depending on how frequently the tape loading was performed. Of course, the interlibrary loan subsystem would continue to be supported by research libraries, which are the greatest potential customers of OCLC's future initiatives.[6] OCLC is already preparing for the shift in use and revenue from their cataloging subsystem to the new products they are developing. These new products such as off-line CD ROM based references or EIDOS (Electronic Information Delivery Online Service) have a greater market potential in the academic research library segment. These kinds of products can be delivered across the local area networks which the research institutions are installing. Due to research libraries heavy reliance on foreign materials, OCLC's entrance in the international market should ultimately also be of greater significance to the research libraries.

COOPERATIVE PROGRAMS

Research libraries do feel a need for cooperative programs in collection management, resource sharing, the development of the CJK terminal, retrospective conversion of records, and preservation. These programs are not necessarily network programs (that is, dependent on electronic technology for their implementation) but they have for the most part been network activities. RLG has taken a leadership role in these areas and has made substantial contributions to the profession in doing so. ARL in its activities has tried to extend these efforts to many more of its member libraries. There continues to be a lack of clarity over OCLC's role in this area among the member research libraries. The regional networks have made some efforts to establish comparable programs but with limited success. At a recent OCLC meeting of research library directors, Robert O'Neil, President of the University of Virginia, proposed eleven ways in which OCLC and RLG might develop closer ties. The changing nature of OCLC and the changing needs of research libraries may yield a new alliance between RLG and OCLC.

SUMMARY

Research libraries will spend the remainder of the decade concentrating on the development of their local systems, and the delivery of library services and information products across their local area networks. In doing so, their nature and needs will diverge from other types of libraries. During this time they will be reluctant participants in multitype networks, and they will find it difficult to support the egalitarian ambitions of the NAC statement on networking. They lend less support to the regional networks in favor of a more direct relationship with OCLC, and the type of services they require from the national utilities will change. Research libraries will become gateways to large numbers of end-users within their own academic communities who will be connected to them via intelligent terminals and they will become key consumers of the new information products that their end-users will expect.

NOTES

1. *Library of Congress Information Bulletin* 46(3), 36 (January 19, 1987).
2. Susan K. Martin, *Governance Issues For Automated Library Networks: The Impact Of, And Implications For, Research Libraries* (Phd. diss., University of California, Berkeley, 1983), p. 125.
3. Barbara M. Robinson, "The Nature of Exchanges Between Libraries In Multitype Cooperatives," *Proceedings, California Conference On Networking September 19-22, 1985* (Belmont 1985), pp. 72-89.
4. Hugh C. Atkinson, "Benefits of Multitype Cooperation," *Proceedings, California Conference On Networking September 19-22, 1985* (Belmont 1985), pp. 15-25.
5. Robert A. Walton, "The 1986 Automated System Marketplace: New Perspectives, New Vistas," *Library Journal*, 112 (April 1, 1987), p. 41.
6. Rowland C. W. Brown, "OCLC and The Future: Collaboration or Fragmentation in a Distributed Environment" (a paper based on a talk presented at the Membership Meeting of the SUNY/OCLC Network, November 21, 1986), p.12.

Networking and Institutional Planning

Donald E. Riggs

Ralph Waldo Emerson used to greet old friends whom he had not seen in a while with the following salutation: "What's become clear to you since we last met?" It has become abundantly clear that products and services of library networks have increased substantially in type and number during the past decade. Libraries and their parent institutions depend significantly on these networking activities to fulfill their mission, and must include them in their planning process.

Library networking is no longer optional; it has become obligatory. Bearing this inescapable fact in mind, library leaders would be prudent to factor the benefits received from networking into their planning process. Participants in networks are required to shift from a "local holdings" attitude to a "shared access" orientation. Some autonomy is surrendered whenever a library joins a network. Moreover, network participation makes the planning process more complex. As the services of networks become more diverse, institutional planning will inherently focus on networking as a means rather than an end.

ENVIRONMENTAL SCANNING

One of the first steps that is required in any formal planning process is an assessment of the institution's internal and external environment. Libraries and their parent institutions have to be proactive in determining which local and outside forces will have an impact on their future and take action to control these forces. WOTS UP (an acronym for weaknesses, opportunities, threats, and strengths underlying planning) is a mechanism used for discovering forces that will have an influence

---

Donald E. Riggs has a BA in Biology from Glenville State College, an MA in Administration from University of West Virginia, an MLS from University of Pittsburgh, and an EdD in Leadership from the University of Colorado. He is currently University Librarian at the Arizona State University. Dr. Riggs is the author of *Strategic Planning for Library Managers* (Oryz Press, 1984).

© 1988 by The Haworth Press, Inc. All rights reserved.

on the future of an organization. Planning's primary purpose is to make provisions to exploit or avoid these forces.

The internal environment is easier to cope with than external factors. One can readily assess the strengths and weaknesses of the existing collections, personnel, services, and technology. Normally, these components are controllable by the library managers. The internal environment of the library can usually be described as one of the following three types:

1. *Stable.* The library is confronted with familiar problems and opportunities. There is an infrequent need for change in the stable environment. This environment fits the bureaucratic organization with risk aversion, centralization, programmed activity, and tight control.
2. *Flexible (through regulation).* Under this type of environment, the library is also confronted with familiar problems and opportunities, but there is a frequent need for change. Regulated flexibility has some decentralization, separate planning, and limited participation in planning.
3. *Adaptive.* The library tends to be confronted with unprecedented problems and opportunities. The adaptive situation fits the library that participates in more risk-taking endeavors, decision-making activities, and with greater emphasis on objectives and results.

It should be understood that every library will not fit exactly into one of these environmental types. These examples simply provide a basis for determining a structure to use when encompassing network services in the library's planning process.

Analysis of the elements of the library's external environment will provide critical information for the planning process as it pertains to network participation. Emerging new technologies are requiring library managers to rethink their existing organizations and services; shrinking and steady state budgets require better planning in redeployment of scarce resources while dealing successfully with a changing library environment. Libraries everywhere are acquiring microcomputers at a time when these machines are undergoing technological improvements almost on a daily basis. It is projected that within the next five years new microcomputers will be five to 10 times more powerful than present day configurations, with 10 to 21 times the active memory and with the graphics capabilities previously available only on costly, specialized systems.

Every eight years computer technology has advanced in performance parameters by the order of one hundred times. Five such periods of advancements may be distinguished historically, and we are now in the sixth, termed the fifth generation. For comparison, the aircraft industry has seen only one such comparable advance in its 75-year history. Other events (e.g., increases in cost for library materials) in the external environment will have an influence on library planning, but none will have the impact that will be realized by emerging technologies. Networks will play an important role in assisting libraries with the new technology. However, library leaders are held responsible for putting technology into the right perspective as it concerns one's local environment. Too often library directors spend time worrying about technology or buffering their library from its undesirable and unintended consequences. These same directors must recognize the competing forces in the external environment and plan with a full range of services in mind. New services will require a different set of skills and resources in order for libraries to compete successfully with external forces and to thrive in the future. Here is where the networks will be greatly appreciated.

GOALS, OBJECTIVES, AND STRATEGIES

In the planning process it is crucial that the library's mission statement is in concurrence with the mission of the parent institution. One would assume that this sense of common direction prevails, but it is absolutely necessary to place the written mission statements side by side for verification. Too many times one learns too late that the library's mission statement does not concur with that of the parent organization. The importance of the mission statement is not to be discounted, since all goals, objectives, and strategies are predetermined by the organization's mission.

Goals. Development of goals for any organization is the official declaration of purpose. A goal is best described as a broad or general statement of desired or intended accomplishment. However, goals must be capable of being converted into specific, measurable objectives. Services realized from networks may not be reflected specifically in a library's goals, but they are most certainly implied. During the goal-setting process the planning committee will undoubtedly consider the resource sharing benefits derived from networks. For example, the goals of the Arizona State University Libraries contain the following three goals that can only be attained through networking:

1. To develop and promote a quality program of resource sharing and alternative access in order to serve the needs of local users and to support the cooperation efforts of libraries in general.
2. To enhance assistance to users in identifying and locating recorded information.
3. To facilitate access to materials other than those in the University Libraries' collections.

As networks diversify, we can expect to find more library goals relating to access and cooperative endeavors. Goals provide a definitive direction and serve as the planning skeleton for integrating all areas of the library into a total library effort.

Objectives. Purposeful, short-termed, measurable, understandable, and verifiable are good adjectives to describe objectives. They can be depicted as the landmarks and milestones which mark the path toward the library's goal(s). Objectives are based on specific goals, but they are more internally focused and imply a resource commitment. By ranking objectives, priorities are established for a given planning year. Following are some examples of objectives based on networking dependence:

1. To improve the "fill" rate of interlibrary loans by 15%.
2. To train 20% of the catalogers how to use the network's new software package.
3. To convert 90,000 catalog records into electronic format by the end of the fiscal year.

Like goals, more objectives can be accomplished via networks as they continue to diversify. Networks as they relate to the fulfillment of objectives should not be described from a mechanical point of view; by doing this we may lose sight of the reason for networks—which is service.

Strategies. After the library has assessed the internal and external environment, revisited its mission statement, developed goals and objectives, then the most important part of the planning process occurs—the formulation of strategies to achieve the goals and objectives. Strategies are best defined as "courses of action." It is noteworthy to differentiate between "tactics" and "strategies." Tactics are plans/activities that are operational (day to day) in nature. Strategies address the broader picture; they are the overall design within which tactical moves are made.

The formulation of strategies is more of an art than a science. Every library has its own strategies, however subtle they may be in the organization. A strategy generally represents a practical choice; it will enable a library to move from where it is today to where it wants to go in the future. Strategy should be viewed as an evaluation of alternatives open to the library and a selection of what appears to be the best course(s) of action to pursue.

Networks provide library managers additional strategies in the process of delivering library services. For example, in order to gain assistance with the implementation of authority control a network can be employed for this purpose. National and regional networks have provided cataloging and interlibrary loan services for several years. Customized catalog service is an example of addressing a specific library's needs. A library may now achieve its strategy of implementing computerized reference service via a regional or national network. Networks are best known for assisting libraries in three major strategy areas:

1. *Opportunistic Strategies*. Libraries and their parent institutions have to keep a constant eye on various ways and means for achieving their goals and objectives. Windows of opportunity should be carefully examined to see if an effective strategy can be formulated, pursued, and attained. Timing is of prime importance while dealing with this type of strategizing. A good example of an opportunistic strategy is that of taking advantage of the network's staff expertise in microcomputer training, especially when the library does not have anyone on its staff with microcomputer expertise.
2. *Innovation Strategies*. Networks have moved rapidly into new and different services and products in recent years. Part of the reason for offering more "innovative" services/products is the competition networks are encountering from private information service brokers and other networks. With its automation specialists, a network can lend substantial assistance with the library's introduction of a new technology strategy. An innovative strategy does not focus on the existing situation or practices. Rather, it is aimed at creating distinguishably new concepts of value and thereby generating a significant impact on the local library environment.
3. *Financial Strategies*. City managers, college/university presidents, and corporation presidents are all expecting the library director to exercise financial accountability and cost effectiveness. What are some strategies that the library director can use to

get the "mostest" from available dollars? A prime example of using networks for getting the greatest "bang from the buck" is that of employing a network to convert the library's card catalog into electronic format. The economics of scale principle reveals that with the larger volume of work performed, there is a reduction in unit costs. Also, the total fixed costs of productive capacity are allocated among a larger number of products (i.e., a network doing retrospective conversion of catalog records for several libraries can do the work cheaper than any one library). Institutions are under pressure to minimize costs. Financial strategies are aplenty in all types of service organizations. Leaders of these organizations are expecting their library directors to seek out and implement ways to lower cost without any erosion of quality. Networks have generally established an excellent performance record in cost effectiveness.

DEPENDENCIES AND EXCHANGES

In the sense of John Donne's words "that no man is an island," a library's ability to deliver information and documents cannot be limited to ownership. Libraries must depend significantly upon effective access to a large universe of resources. With steady state and shrinking materials budgets, we will witness greater dependency by libraries on one another's collections. Institutions should not at any time reduce materials budgets because their libraries have created a dependency on other collections within a network. In some local networks and consortia (e.g., the Colorado Alliance of Research Libraries), cooperative acquisitions programs have been implemented. In arrangements of this nature individual libraries build on specific collection strengths (e.g., if one library holds substantive holdings in architecture, then the other libraries in the cooperative endeavor will most likely refrain from purchasing a large number of volumes in architecture). This type of cooperative acquisitions program must be orchestrated and evaluated on a regular basis. It will play a determining role in planning, budgeting, and analyzing collections. There is an inherent danger that the library's parent organization may put too much emphasis on the cooperative acquisitions endeavor and not provide adequate funding for the local collection. It is incumbent upon the library director to convince the organization's leadership that the basic premise of a cooperative acquisitions program will fail if planning for the infusion of appropriate funds at the local level for books, journals, and microforms does not occur. Dependencies on networks and consortia must be fully comprehended by the library directors' superiors. Some libraries have suffered financially due to misunderstandings about the role of networks.

Understanding the theory of exchange among libraries is crucial when institutions enter into network agreements. The exchange theory is at its best when two or more libraries decide to interact for the purpose of deriving mutual benefits (e.g., resource sharing). Networks and their participating members must prevent the creation of a "greenback curtain" that separates those libraries who can afford to pay for information from those who cannot. If there is one illness to which the library profession is susceptible, it is the tendency to make Byzantine what is essentially Arcadian. It would be prudent for library directors to explain the difference to their institution's leaders.

DIVERSITIES

The changing technology requires much attention and careful planning. Institutions responsible for libraries tend to depend largely on the library director to dovetail library planning with institutional planning; this is particularly true for those components of the planning process addressing technology. Does the library's local area network coincide with the city's LAN? Will the library's new circulation system interact with the university's computerized personnel records? These are the types of questions that should generate close coordination and planning between the library and its institution's various departments. Networks can perhaps play a role in the coordination and planning. Networks are no longer simply a broker of access to bibliographic records. Services offered by networks include training/assistance with new software applications, implementation of local area networks, preparation of databases for local automation projects, conducting workshops on new technologies, and equipment procurement. Regional and national networks will continue to offer more diversified services. CD-ROM and advanced laser/optical technologies are examples of areas in which networks are already working and offering to their members.

COOPERATIVE, SYSTEMATIC PLANNING

Too often planning is done in isolation. For example, if one were to examine the long-range plan for the city, it would not be uncommon to find conflicting paths toward the attainment of similar conceptual goals. Annual planning retreats have eliminated some of this type of conflicting focus on the future. Planning is not an attempt to read tea leaves and outwit the future. However, the library and its parent institution can identify likelihoods, built-in dynamics, and even a few near-certainties that will occur in their collective future. Competition from the external environment has dictated that the respective library and institutional leaders become more proactive in their approach to planning. Effective planning asserts that neither willfulness nor acquiescence to the fashions and contemporary external conditions is an appropriate course for an institution and its library. Planning cannot be passive, but must be very proactive and purposeful.

The library director would be remiss if the role of networks were not factored into the planning process. The benefits of network participation must be stated in specific terms, not vague and vapid. Definitive attention has to be given to the role of networks in local library and institutional planning; the role of networks has to be coupled with an overall institutional strategy. Planning for network involvement cannot be treated as a phantasmagoria about tomorrow. Networks will enhance the possibility of having a secure future for one's institution and library if they are planned for in a rational, analytical manner. Thus, through systematic planning of the integration of a network's contributions toward the attainment of the library's and its institution's goals/objectives, a "win-win" situation will prevail.

CONCLUSION

All types of public and private institutions providing library service must ask the following three basic questions before engaging in any planning process: What is our business? What will our business be? What should our business be? Answers to these questions will provide the foundation upon which goals, objectives, and strategies can be formulated. Planning is required to undergo a metamorphosis from being reactive in nature to a process that is more strategically future-oriented. After the question about what should our business be is answered, then a planning process has to be put into place to make the desired "business" happen.

Unquestionably, networks have proven that they can help a library create its future. The benefits realized from a network have caused libraries and their parent institutions to rethink strategic directions to be taken to attain established goals and objectives. With greater diversification of services and products expected from networks, libraries will depend even more on networks. The role of networks will become more prominent in the library's long-range planning process. Networks will enable libraries to espouse new alertness, greater flexibility for new opportunities, and stronger strategic initiatives. Libraries failing to capitalize on the benefits of networks will not "reflect the spirit of the times," but will continue to stand in the doorway of debate about networks. Networks are here to stay, let's use them judiciously for improving user service. Networks most certainly have supported our contention that "we've got connections."

Ownership of Bibliographic Data and Its Importance to Consortia

Charles B. Lowry

IMPORTANCE OF THE DATABASE

Recent experience indicates that there are two capital expenditures which libraries will sustain as they exploit automation to carry out basic library functions. The purchase of hardware and software systems is one, and the construction of their bibliographic database is the other. Gradually the cost for systems has been accepted as one which libraries may expect to sustain repeatedly. The widespread notion is that about every five to ten years the Library will go through the process of "vendor abandonment," to use the accepted euphemism for changing to a different local system.[1]

By contrast, preparation of a database, which is likely to be more costly than system acquisitions, may not be a recurring cost if the library safeguards its database in two important and fundamentally different ways. A library's machine-readable records must follow standard bibliographic format (MARC) and have the appropriate supporting authority control, as well as linked records for holdings, circulation, acquisitions, and similar functional needs. These safeguards are largely dependent on the effectiveness of the library's own technical services and the vendors from whom the library acquires machine-readable records and external technical support. Equally important to a library is safeguarding its freedom to use the database in new ways. If the library's ownership of its machine-readable database is in any way circumscribed by external control, then the library may be subjected to continuous and repetitive costs in the reuse of its data and limited in the cooperative efforts it might wish to make with other libraries. In-

---

Charles B. Lowry is currently Director of Libraries, University of Texas at Arlington. He holds an MSLS from UNC/Chapel Hill and a PhD in History from the University of Florida. He has served as a member of the SOLINET Board and as Chair of the SOLINET/OCLC Contract Committee. He also has represented AMIGOS on the OCLC Users Council. He is currently Associate Editor of *Library Administration and Management*.

© 1988 by The Haworth Press, Inc. All rights reserved.

deed, depending on the limitations a bibliographic utility can exercise on the use of derived data, a library might find itself faced with permanent licensing fees and restrictions on cooperative activities with local or state-wide library consortia, not to mention other vendors and regional or national networks. There is one rule to follow in this matter—"Protect your bibliographic data: it may be your most important investment."[2]

NINETEENTH CENTURY NOTIONS AND TWENTIETH CENTURY TECHNOLOGY

Virtually every commentator has observed that technology has outrun our institutional arrangements and practices, our systems for protecting intellectual property rights, and our legal practice, with respect to the use and reuse of all types of electronic data. Put in its simplest terms, the issue is—does a library own the bibliographic records it contributes to or acquires from a utility, and may it choose to use them as it sees fit when new and previously unforeseen opportunities for cooperation arise due to the development of new institutional relationships or new technologies?[3] Prior to the development of on-line bibliographic utilities, the issues being dealt with here simply did not exist.

Certainly, no one challenged the ownership of library catalogs when they existed basically in paper form on cards. Libraries, particularly large libraries, often freely contributed copies of their catalog records to union catalogs, with the clear understanding and expectation that the information was very likely going to be reused. In fact, copies of records were contributed specifically so that other libraries could use the information. Question of ownership or rights to use the records rarely, if ever, surfaced.[4]

Libraries have entered into shared cataloging activities for over a century. As early as the 1850s, Charles Jewett proposed the use of current technologies to reproduce catalog information. With the advent of the Library of Congress printed card activity in 1901, and the development of the National Union Catalog in the same year, shared cataloging became a way of life. The development of on-line bibliographic utilities in the past twenty years has been seen by most librarians as a logical extension of these long established cooperative cataloging activities.[5] "While individual records are created routinely by library staffs and contributed to the utilities as part of a longstanding tradition of shared cataloging, the utilities in turn provide . . . organizational resources to maintain these large files and service the needs of their members. . . ."[6] Librarians have clung to the notion that utilities, especially those that have been created by librarians, are extensions of cooperative practices that existed prior to the application of computers. These relationships can result in serious problems, however, if a library wishes to change utilities or the utility wishes to limit the libraries' access to records in the files.[7]

Most libraries joined a bibliographic utility to improve cataloging productivity rather than for the express purpose of creating machine-readable records.[8] Herein lies the source of our current discontent, for once created, the machine-readable bibliographic record has astonishing potential for reuse in the context of numerous electronic technologies. A digression into the future of library-applied information technologies is germane. Let us envision a hypothetical library which has been cataloging with a major bibliographic utility for fifteen years and has completed the retrospective conversion of its catalog, acquiring records from the utility and from other commercial vendors, as well as LC.

Let us presume further that this library has a fully functional local automated system which includes gateways through the on-line catalog to bibliographic databases and other geographically proximate libraries, some of which catalog on another bibliographic utility. Finally, let us assume that our hypothetical library has acquired various numeric and bibliographic databases for local patron use and loaded these on optical mass storage peripherals geared to main-frame computers (e.g., Kodak Optical Disk System 6800 with a capacity in excess of one terabyte) which can be accessed through its local system and by extension from the other libraries to which it is linked. In addition, this library is now acquiring monograph and journal material on "Laser Cards" (which contain full MARC citations) and provides the means to patrons for copying these cards to use with their own lap-readers. This hypothetical library is a member of a local multi-type library consortium of twenty libraries, all of which have linked local systems and which have for sometime been sharing cataloging information for retrospective conversion purposes.

This vision of the future gives some notion of the potential richness of library information services made possible by modern electronics. Obviously, the machine-readable bibliographic record taken from a utility's member-created database is but one component in a larger and extremely complex picture. What would happen if the bibliographic utility could require the member library to police the use of its bibliographic records and ensure that the utility was "properly compensated" for reuse? Given the numerous sources of the same bibliographic information and the multiple access to it in our hypothetical library, the practical obstacles to this "policing obligation" would be momentous. The library would have little choice but to limit access. Generally, libraries do not consider the plethora of the potential future uses or reuses of their records.

Such future uses might include withdrawal of the file from a shared local commercial or utility system for mounting on a competing system; duplication of a subset of the file on a different support system for a special purposes union list; or contributing the file to a shared automated system to support cataloging and/or conversion by other libraries.[9]

The only certainty is that libraries will seek to use these bibliographic records, acquired at great expense from the shared cataloging file of the utility, in numerous and unforeseeable ways. It is only reasonable that a library should take steps to safeguard this investment and insure that future uses are not inhibited.

RECORD OWNERSHIP AND USE—
CURRENT PRACTICE BY UTILITIES

Two fundamentally different approaches have been used by bibliographic utilities and vendors in dealing with the issues that arise from reuse of bibliographic data. UTLAS, BIBLIOFILE, MARCIVE and Research Libraries Group (RLG) have each taken the stance that the library may reuse data once acquired without restriction or further remuneration. Western Library Network (WLN), REMARC, and the On-line Computerized Library Center (OCLC) have each taken a fundamentally different approach to the reuse of records by libraries. This approach is characterized by the establishment of restrictions on reuse of records, albeit each uses slightly different mechanisms. These controls clearly arise out of a concern for maximizing profit and protecting the database from use by third parties for profit.

At the present time, there is an increasing number of sources for machine-readable bibliographic data, and most do not place any serious restrictions on reuse of records.[10] The Library of Congress, long the major supplier of shared MARC cataloging records, has continued to maintain a policy of basically free distribution of its records to U.S. libraries with absolutely no restrictions on reuse since they are in the "public domain." The first modification of this longstanding practice occurred in 1985, when LC began to claim copyright on its records outside of the United States. In 1986, LC informed all eighty MARC distribution service customers involved in foreign markets that wholesale redistribution by any agency other than LC outside the U.S. was prohibited. This practice will not have an appreciable affect on American libraries if effective agreements on international exchange of MARC records are worked out.

Several commercial vendors depend primarily or solely upon LC MARC records. The BIBLIOFILE Database comes from LC MARC, and BIBLIOFILE makes no attempt to restrain the use of data extracted from the disks that it distributes in its retrospective conversion services. Because BIBLIOFILE has no member input as yet, anticipated policy for such data has not been completely developed. Likewise, MARCIVE has developed a database composed primarily of records derived from LC, NLM, USGPO, and Canadian MARC. Libraries acquiring records from MARCIVE are free to use them in any way they see fit and reuse or redistribute records as well. MARCIVE has an "original input database," but it is not shared by MARCIVE customers and, as yet, there is no need to establish a "record use" policy on this database.

In 1984, UTLAS moved to the "for-profit" sector when it was acquired by Thomson Limited. UTLAS records are by Canadian law copyrighted at the time they are created. This presents potential dilemmas for customers which UTLAS eliminates by its licensing agreements. UTLAS views its customers' databases derived from original input and records copied from other databases to which UTLAS provides access as the property of the customer. "Customers own the records they create through UTLAS facilities. The records may be loaded for the customer's use into other automated systems which the customer may own or license, or to which it subscribes."[11] Through this straightforward, if simple mechanism, UTLAS protects its own use of the copyrighted information in its database and allows customers free and unfettered use of records that they acquire from UTLAS.

RLG maintains a service agreement which is considerably more liberal than other "non-profit" utilities. In the first place, unlike OCLC and WLN, RLG members are not required to do all current cataloging on the RLIN System, but are encouraged to participate as fully as possible without a requirement to purchase any minimal amount of RLIN services. Members may use records they input into the database or copy from it "for any purpose whatsoever." In addition, "all records added to the RLIN Database by the institution are permanently and without restriction contributed to such database, and may be used by RLG for any purpose whatsoever."[12] Thus, RLG like UTLAS has provided for members to use and reuse records in the database without restrictions, while at the same time preserving its own freedom to develop and market new uses of the RLIN Database.

WLN claims ownership to the bibliographic database which it "compiles and organizes." WLN retains the right to transfer, or otherwise use the member input records, to "not-for-profit systems provided that the recipient system reciprocate by making records in their databases available to WLN . . . (but) the member shall not itself enter into such data exchange arrangements. The member agrees that the Commission (WLN) may sell the bibliographic database . . . to any licensee of the WLN software." WLN in turn allows members to enter records from the database into the local systems used only by WLN members without restriction. Members may enter records into local systems used by nonmembers subject to WLN's "cluster membership policy," which is waived in cases where nonmembers contribute their records to the local system from another source. WLN allows no distribution of records by members to third parties in machine-readable form without prior written permission, except the members' own original input. In addition, members are required to use the WLN Database for all current cataloging, including original and copy cataloging. The WLN "principal member agreement" does not make provision for cases in which a member might wish to move to another bibliographic utility. Under the terms of the "Agreement," the member would need the permission of WLN to move its records into another bibliographic utility and, by a logical extension, permission to move to another bibliographic utility.[13]

The REMARC Database is an example of print format bibliographic information which was originally in the public domain. The Carrollton Press conversion of this manual file created machine-readable records which are not in the public domain. The REMARC database is marketed with strict controls over reuse to ensure the future market which is presently about fifty cents per record. REMARC requires that libraries which purchase records enter into an agreement whereby the library may freely transfer printed eye-readable versions of the records and up to half of the characters of an individual record in machine-readable form, but not in any case is the library allowed to transfer a whole machine-readable record to a third party which has not entered into an agreement with REMARC concerning the reuse of records. All print and machine records so transferred must contain a REMARC identifier code. REMARC does allow the library to provide access to records that it has acquired for normal uses such as reference, ILL and on-line public access catalogs. The basic usage restrictions of the REMARC agreement do accommodate many reuses of the records which libraries find desirable such as union catalogs. However, the libraries must negotiate before they mount REMARC records on local automated systems which might be accessed for cataloging purposes by other libraries.[14]

Until recently, the chief method for establishing restrictions on the reuse of machine-readable records has been through contract and licensing agreements. In the one case where a specific copyright on a database existed, UTLAS eschewed its implied copyright control by licensing libraries to reuse records freely. In December of 1982, the OCLC Board made the fateful decision to apply for a copyright of the OCLC database, transforming the situation which had previously existed. That application had been preceded by public hearings as early as 1979 which were repeated at ALA Midwinter in 1985. OCLC has staunchly defended the decision to file a registry of copyright, in spite of more or less universal opposition to this action in the library community, including a direct request by OCLC User's Council that means other than copyright be used to protect the database from unauthorized third-party use.[15]

It is not possible to describe in summary fashion the contractual arrangements which OCLC maintains with various regional and state networks, because OCLC establishes different agreements with each. These agreements, to a great extent, depend on OCLC's ability and the network's ability to cut the best deal they can, which is a function of the size of the regionals' membership, their varying technical capacities, and their ability and desire to provide non-OCLC services. Moreover, OCLC and its affiliated networks have been involved in extended and unsuccessful contract negotiations since early 1983, which have been compounded by OCLC's contemporaneous registry of copyright. The networks maintained a united front in these negotiations, asserting the need for a "core contract" common to all networks, and at least six drafts were produced.

In 1986, OCLC was able to achieve its longstanding objective of independent negotiations with each network. Subsequent negotiations have resulted in but a single contract between OCLC and ILLINET.[16] Whatever the outcome of the contract negotiations, many observers believe that copyright has provided a foundation on which OCLC has asserted rights in the database, exceeding any that could be established in copyright law,[17] a fact observable in reading several versions of the "Network Core Contract" and the "Principles and Guidelines for Transfer of OCLC Derived Machine-Readable Records, Revision of May 13, 1986." The outcome of the interlocking issue of contract and copyright is of profound importance to the library community simply because literally thousands of libraries participate in OCLC services.

OPENING PANDORA'S BOX – THE UNCERTAIN EFFECTS OF OCLC'S COPYRIGHT

Many librarians, perhaps most, have felt that the OCLC copyright registry is a violation of the spirit of cooperation in which the library community has operated in building the OCLC Union Catalog. Whether or not this is true is now a moot point. What is more important is the significant problems which will arise in the interpretation and enforcement of copyright law. Libraries are likely to be drawn into the increasingly litigious world of the information industry which has experienced a rise from around 600 cases in 1981 to over 5,000 in 1985.[18]

When considering the effects of OCLC's filing, there are several salient facts to remember. LC registered OCLC's copyright claim in March, 1984, because there was a *prima facie* case for its validity, but LC's Copyright Office narrowed the claim to a compilation of the online database. This raises considerable question about whether OCLC can restrict use of offline products, such as archive tapes or records copied individually from the database. The Office also noted that it only registers claims; the courts rule on their validity; and that other parties who have input data may wish to register as co-authors of the OCLC database. Over twenty libraries and AMIGOS, an OCLC affiliated network, have since made copyright filings, which in one way or another limit OCLC's claim.

Copyright presents a significant and complex new obstacle to the achievement of contractual agreements. Virtually all commentators on the OCLC copyright registration (including OCLC Board and Management as well as members of the library community) have emphasized the importance of preserving the economic asset of the OCLC database, built through the common effort of library participants. Libraries have considered the role of OCLC to be that of an instrumentality performing a work for hire.[19] Indeed, members of the OCLC Board and management have consistently cited their "fiduciary responsibility" in explaining their decision to copyright. Unfortunately, copyright does not have as one of its primary goals the preservation of the economic interests of the author but rather the common good. "Under the law, the government is authorized to grant intellectual property rights not as rewards but as inducements to authors and inventors to create and to disseminate intellectual works."[20] Given this longstanding constitutional and legal principle, it is at least arguable that an *exclusive* copyright of the OCLC database inhibits the library participants from adding to that database.[21]

However, the case law in these matters is incomplete and equivocal, if not contradictory. Present intellectual property laws provide two forms of protection—patents and copyright. The former requires that the protected design be disclosed and the latter is based on the assumption that in order to gain profit, the author will publish. These protections reflect the basic differences between inventions based on patent prevention of commercial use and writings based on copyright prevention of commercial copying.[22] Congress has not included databases specifically in the protection of recent copyright legislation. However, in considering the closely related matter of computer programs the Congress expressed its intention specifically to "avoid extending copyright beyond the writing or expression of ideas in the program so as to protect processes or methods . . . , and thus the long-standing prohibition against protection of ideas was specifically codified."[23]

Copyright legislation and case law have repeatedly emphasized the principle that "facts themselves are in the public domain, available to all, and are thus not copyrightable, but compilations of facts may precede copyright protection." OCLC filed for specific protection of the database as a compilation, which is a subset of a general category of copyrightable material known as "collective works." Historically, the courts have taken two views for the protection of such compilations. The interest being protected in the older view was the labor and effort of the compiler, the so-called "sweat-of-the-brow copyright." More recently courts have seen the "selection and arrangement of data as the *indica* of the originality of the work and thus, its copyrightability."[24] When protecting "sweat copyright" the courts have generally followed the reasoning that the use of another's data to save time and effort, even where the data has been rearranged, is an infringement.

Where the courts have found infringement of copyright by the use of the selection and arrangement of facts, it is necessary to prove extensive copying of that arrangement to sustain an infringement case.[25] OCLC can best protect the individual bibliographic records from reuse by accepting participating libraries as co-authors but will have to prove copying of a substantial portion of the arrangement under the "sweat" copyright principle in order to restrict member libraries, participating networks, and third parties from using "facts" from the OCLC database.

There are numerous interrelated problems in protecting intellectual property rights through the traditional means of copyright. These are the problems of identifying authorship, actual infringement, private use, functional use, derivative use, intangible works, educational goals, artistic integrity, and international use.[26] Examining these problems in some detail illustrates the potentially insidious effects of copyright as a means of protecting the OCLC database. Any reading of the published literature on the "copyrightability" of bibliographic databases gives the clear perspective that the legal issues are open to diametrically opposed interpretations and that the resolution of these problems may well be in the hands of courts and lawyers for years to come, unless the library community can resolve the obstacles presented by copyright through cross-licensing and contract agreements. Moreover, in the absence of resolution the inevitable copyright cases may well have results which no parties to the dispute may wish. In addition, the OCLC filing has resulted in a trickle of additional copyright filings which may turn into a deluge if agreements are not reached.

In general, it has been accepted that if databases are copyrightable it would be as "compilations" under U.S. Copyright law. But this notion can be subjected to serious legal scrutiny. A compilation is defined as an original work of authorship created by collecting and assembling pre-existing data which is "selected, coordinated, or arranged" to result in a new work. Moreover, compilations are a subset of a general category known as "collective works" in which a number of independently copyrightable works are assembled to form a new work. In a compilation, the assembled data are not independently copyrightable. This distinction is subtle but important to the analysis of the ownership of bibliographic and other computer databases. If the assembled materials are not individually copyrightable, then the database is a compilation and the bibliographic utility need not concern itself with obtaining consent of the individual libraries to use and reuse the records input. In this case, a utility could limit all uses of the data by libraries and third parties except those that fall under the "Fair Use" principle. On the other hand, if bibliographic databases are collective works, then the current cooperative organizational schemes on which bibliographic databases are built would be tenable only by arranging a contractual definition of rights with each participant either transferring his/her copyright or granting a right for unrestricted use to other participants.[27]

Fairly detailed and strong arguments have been made that the individual bibliographic records created in the library cataloging process meet all of the requirements of "fixation, authorship, and originality" and that "it appears quite certain that the catalog record is copyrightable as an original work of authorship fixed in the necessary tangible form." In this case, the individual libraries would be the copyright holders since catalogers work for hire, and the employer is considered the author for purposes of the statute.[28] It seems certain then that databases are copyrightable either as collective works or as compilations, and it was certainly the intent of Congress to allow copyright protection for those databases which could be defined as compilations.[29]

Even if individual records were declared "facts" instead of copyrightable information, bibliographic databases would be copyrightable as compilations only if they also meet the required tests. One of the primary tests will be that of originality which has been established in case law based on the principle of "industrious collection" ("sweat-of-the-brow copyright"), the extent of judgment exercised by the compiler in selecting data for inclusion in the compilation, or the manner in which the data are arranged by the compiler. Thus, collection, selection, and arrangement constitute possible justifications for originality, but they have been applied in different ways at different times. "Bibliographic computer databases, however, are significantly different from traditional compilations, and even from other computer databases, in ways that could lead to a different result, particularly if the claim of sole authorship is made by bibliographic utility."[30]

Bibliographic utilities do not actively collect the data, but rather receive it passively from libraries, nor do they create, discover, or in any meaningful sense select bibliographic records. To the extent that these activities go on, it is participating libraries which supply the effort. It is also arguable that utilities do not create the arrangement of the records in the traditional sense of compiling, but that arrangements are merely the results of the technical requirements of computers. However, it is possible to make an argument that software of a utility constitutes a sort of functional equivalent of the traditional arranging. "The utilities, then, demonstrate at best a highly attenuated form of original authorship."[31] Nevertheless, the limits of copyright law have been extended and authorship redefined when the primary purposes of copyright law have been fostered by a new form of authorship. As discussed above, the purpose of copyright is not financial reward to the author, but the encouragement of the growth of new ideas and expression which are in the public interest. Obviously the creation of bibliographic databases is in the public interest but granting exclusive copyright and monopolistic control may not encourage their growth.

CLOSING PANDORA'S BOX

These dilemmas in the application of copyright to bibliographic databases have been raised by the OCLC filing. The answers will emerge only when a suit is brought against the registration of that copyright, or when OCLC sues an institution claiming copyright on a database of records, some of which are derived from the OCLC database. The research by Richard Brown and Celia Delano Moore, which has been relied on heavily in these pages, suggests two possible solutions. "While the fit is not perfect, bibliographic databases appear to be potentially copyrightable as joint works . . . (which) would allow for copyright protection of the databases without altering the existing definition of authorship." The cost would be that any of the joint authors might license use by non-participating third parties which in effect would destroy copyright protection.

This problem can be gotten around largely by the contractual restriction on the right of joint-authors to grant licenses without prior approval.[32] The second approach argues that once a library acquires machine-readable bibliographic data by copying it from a database (whether on archive tapes or by direct electronic transfer) then it is within the fair use provisions of the copyright law for the library to use the records so acquired in any way that it sees fit. Even the largest ARL libraries would not be copying the arrangement of a significant portion of a utility's database, and thus, would not be in violation of copyright on a compilation, even if they transferred the records to a third-party vendor who later used them for profit.[33]

Imbedded in both of these alternatives are significant legal issues which will probably never be resolved outside of the courtroom, unless OCLC were to agree that participating libraries were joint authors by filing for registry of copyright in their behalf or encouraging them to do so. Under the present circumstances, litigation is not only possible, but highly likely. If this outcome is to be avoided, libraries and local consortia will perforce take a more assertive stance concerning the use of records issue. They must view *all* bibliographic utilities with the same care that they do now with the suppliers of library systems and software. To protect their own futures and the large investments that they make in creating databases, they must develop contractual relationships which include a number of provisions:

—rights to non-exclusive ownership in the data purchased;
—unlimited rights to share the data with other libraries without payment of royalties or other fees;
—unlimited rights to transfer the data from one agency vendor to another for any purpose specified by the library;
—unlimited rights to use or the data in any format, including machine-readable record.[34]

Recently, the release by OCLC of the "Principles and Guidelines" has moved in the direction of qualifying its claims to exclusive control of the database through copyright. However, that document is flawed in several significant ways which, unless changed, make it useless for achieving the needs of libraries and library consortia. In the first place, OCLC agrees not to invoke copyright against member libraries, but only if they execute a contract incorporating the "Principles and Guidelines." Libraries are allowed to transfer records to other member libraries and use these records "without restriction." However, libraries are not permitted to transfer records to member networks, local consortia, or state library agencies unless these enter into specific agreements with OCLC. This means that libraries may not, without OCLC's consent, enter into arrangements for resource sharing, (e.g., ILL, retrospective conversion, union catalogs, etc.) with the organizations which must serve as the instrumentalities for that resource sharing.

In short, a strict construction of the "Principles and Guidelines" allows libraries to use their records in any way they wish so long as they do not work through the organizations which would actually allow them to do so. The "Principles and Guidelines" also includes a clause which allows OCLC to modify them unilaterally while they are in effect as part of a current contract. For obvious reasons, this would be unacceptable to a contracting member. Moreover, the "Principles and Guidelines" does not eschew the use of copyright litigation against member networks, library systems (consortia), or state library agencies, and specifically requires such agencies to develop separate understandings with OCLC on the use of transferred records.

Finally, it is ironic that "upon termination of its membership in OCLC, a former member library may transfer records of its holdings, without restriction to any third party from which the library elects to obtain bibliographic cataloging services."[35] In effect, it would appear that a library would have more freedom to use its records by leaving OCLC than remaining a contributing member.

CONCLUSION

It has been argued herein that the use of copyright to protect the OCLC Database was a mistaken way of protecting from commercial third-party use a valuable asset of the library community developed by member participation. On the other hand, it may be an effective strategy for limiting local library consortia and OCLC affiliated networks from developing library services and products which OCLC deems competitive with its own future marketing intentions. Short of OCLC withdrawing its copyright, or filing for joint authorship for member libraries, it is likely that the next phase of the copyright debate will be conducted in courts.

The best available means for avoiding the centrifugal effects of litigation is for OCLC, its affiliated networks, and member libraries to adopt the practice of contractual cross-licensing as a means to protect the database and at the same time allow libraries, affiliated networks, and consortia the freedom necessary to continue developing this rich bibliographic resource which they have built in concert. There is evidence that OCLC will increasingly attempt to limit the reuses of records by its member libraries and networks. A natural result will be for members to look for alternative sources of cataloging and cooperation which will not restrict the full exploitation of a libraries catalog records. However, OCLC could follow the lead of the "for-profit" UTLAS which licenses its customers to reuse records from a copyrighted database or the "not-for-profit" RLG which has declined to apply for copyright and, through contracts, licenses its members to use the records acquired as they see fit without surrendering copyright as a means of limiting use of its data by competitors outside of the OCLC family.

In any event, all libraries and library consortia must be vigilant in protecting their freedom to reuse their own cataloging records, whatever the source of the data. The best means for assuring the needed protection is a carefully prepared contractual agreement with the bibliographic utility or vendor.

NOTES

1. Gary S. Lawrence, Joseph R. Matthews, and Charles E. Miller, "Costs and Features of Online Catalogs: the State of the Art," *Information Technology and Libraries* (December, 1983), pp. 444-45.
2. *Ibid.*
3. See, for instance, Susan K. Martin, *Library Networks, 1986-87: Libraries in Partnership* (White Plains, New York and London: Knowledge Industry Publications, Inc., 1986), pp. 5, 16-17, 24-25, 34-35, 37-38, 144-45.

4. Edward R. Johnson and Louella V. Wetherbee, "Record Ownership Requirements in Local Data Bases for Integrated Library Systems," *Conference on Integrated Online Library Systems Proceedings*, David C. Gemaway, ed. (Canfield, Ohio: Gemaway and Associates, Inc.), p. 437.

5. Celia Delano Moore, "Ownership of Access Information: Exploring the Application of Copyright Law to Library Catalog Records," *Computer/Law Journal*, 4 (Fall, 1983), pp. 321-24.

6. Duane Webster and Lenore S. Maruyama, "Ownership and Distribution of Bibliographic Data: Highlights of a Meeting Held by the Library of Congress Network Advisory Committee (March 4-5, 1980) Working Document" (Washington, D.C.: Library of Congress Network Development Office, December, 1980), p. 5.

7. *Ibid.*

8. American Library Association, "'Ownership' of Machine-Readable Records: A Neglected Consideration in Retrospective Conversion," *Library Systems Newsletter*. 4 (June, 1984), p. 43.

9. *Ibid.*, p. 44.

10. A survey early in 1987 by the author indicates that there is no substantive change in the publicly announced policies and practices of the vendors discussed herein.

11. "UTLAS Policy on Record Ownership, November, 1986."

12. "RLIN Service Agreement, May, 1985."

13. "WLN Principle Member Agreement."

14. A.L.A., "Ownership," p. 44.

15. Rowland C. Brown, et al; "The Ownership of Bibliographic Data—OCLC's Experience: A Symposium," *Journal of Academic Librarianship*, 11 (September, 1985), pp. 197, 200, 201, 202; and American Library Association, "Copyright Hearing at ALA," *Library Systems Newsletter*, 5 (February, 1985), pp. 13-16.

16. During three years of "Core Contract" negotiations at least six drafts were produced which illustrate the depth of disagreement between OCLC and its affiliated regional networks. At the time these negotiations broke down significant differences which remained unresolved included: (1) The right of OCLC to increase prices during the term of the contract; (2) Uniformity of pricing to Networks; (3) The term of the contract and right to termination at will; (4) Network rights to handle the distribution of new OCLC products; and (5) The use and transfer of OCLC-derived machine-readable records, by General Members, Networks, and OCLC. See "Network Report on Core Provisions Where Agreement With OCLC Was Not Yet Reached," February, 1986; and "[OCLC] Report of Contract Negotiations, 1986, February 3." These documents are summaries of meetings held between the Network Contract Committee and OCLC representatives in Atlanta on January 17 and in Chicago on January 20, 1986. The two documents are in essential agreement about the areas of disagreement. No further negotiations on the "Core Contract" were held and by the summer independent negotiations between the Networks and OCLC were emerging as the next phase in negotiations.

17. See, for instance, Rowland C. W. Brown, et al., pp. 199, 203, 205.

18. Mark L. Goldstein, "Meet the New Entrepreneur: Lawyers Must Sort Out Who Owns—and Is Liable for—Electronic Data," *Industry Week* (April 28, 1986), p. 65.

19. A.L.A., "Ownership," pp. 45-46; Dennis D. McDonald, Eleanor Jo Rodger and Jeffrey L. Squires, "Findings of the IFLA International Study on the Copyright of Bibliographic Records in Machine-Readable Form," *IFLA Journal*, 9 (September, 1983), p. 219; Rowland C. W. Brown, et al., p. 202; and Webster, pp. 5, 15.

20. Rowland C. W. Brown, et al., p. 201; and Office of Technology Assessment, *Intellectual Property Rights in an Age of Electronics and Information* (Washington, D.C.: U.S. Congress, Office of Technology Assessment, 1986), p. 7.

21. Richard L. Brown, "Copyright and Computer Databases: The Case of the Bibliographic Utility," *Rutgers Computer and Technology Law Journal*, 11 (Spring, 1985), pp. 43-44.

22. Office of Technology Assessment, p. 11

23. I. Fred Koenigsberg, ed. *Current Developments in Copyright Law, 1986* (New York: Practicing Law Institute, 1986), p. 460.

24. *Ibid.*, pp. 507-08.

25. *Ibid.*, p. 510; and McDonald, p. 213.

26. Office of Technology Assessment, pp. 10-13.

27. Richard L. Brown, pp. 23-26.

28. Moore, pp. 307-15; and Richard L. Brown, pp. 27-36.

29. Moore, p. 336.

30. Richard L. Brown, pp. 36-40.

31. *Ibid.*, p. 42.

32. *Ibid.*, pp. 46-48.

33. Moore, pp. 351-72.

34. Sally Drew, "Online Databases: Some Questions of Ownership," *Wilson Library Bulletin* (June, 1985), p. 661.

35. "Principles and Guidelines for Transfer of OCLC-Derived Machine-Readable Records," revision of May 13, 1986.

The Future of Networks and OCLC

Irene B. Hoadley

INTRODUCTION

Perhaps the title of this paper should have been "To Be or Not To Be" because that really is the question. Will there be a relationship between OCLC and the regional networks or not and if so what kind? Going back to the inception of OCLC in 1967, an early occurrence shaped the character of OCLC. Almost from the beginning libraries outside of Ohio wanted to participate in the activity that was OCLC. What occurred in an evolutionary way was a bipartite structure for the creation and dissemination of OCLC services. The staff of OCLC determined the directions and developed the services which were to be provided. However, OCLC did not disseminate those services to libraries, but instead regional networks that affiliated with OCLC provided the services to libraries. In the beginning this was a mutually beneficial arrangement, but it did often mean that libraries tended to identify with networks rather than OCLC.

As both OCLC and the regional networks continued to grow, a series of differences began to surface. These differences were inevitable as both OCLC and the regional networks began to mature and wanted to assert their independence. Although there are differences, it is still quite obvious that OCLC and the regional networks need each other. In the same way, the need for cooperation in the profession grows, not lessens, and that need will continue to be present for many years to come. What follows is my personal vision (not that of the institution I represent, of AMIGOS, or of OCLC) of how OCLC and the regional networks can coexist and evolve to meet the expectations of the future. Meeting expectations will not be easy because there are various expectations which must be satisfied: those of OCLC; those of the networks;

Irene B. Hoadley is Director of the Sterling C. Evans Library of Texas A & M University. Her degrees are: BA in English, University of Texas; AMLS, University of Michigan; MA in History, Kansas State University, and PhD, University of Michigan. A former chair of the OCLC Users' Council, Dr. Hoadley is currently a member of the OCLC Board.

and those of libraries. The real question is whether all of the needs and expectations can be satisfied in a single solution or even in several solutions. The real crux, however, is that there must be a level of cooperation because none of the major players can afford the luxury of not cooperating.

The first question which should be asked is whether there is a future which continues the interrelationships of OCLC and the regional networks. It would be foolish to think otherwise. OCLC and the regional networks need each other. Looking at the relationship from the simplest level, it would be hard for either to do what they do without the other. The regional networks are, in one dimension, the service or distribution units of OCLC. They promote services, train users and maintain an ongoing relationship with general members. OCLC creates services through research, development and implementation, and the regional networks then take those services and make them available to libraries. On the surface this is a clear-cut relationship which operates on the same basis as car manufacturers and dealers.

EVOLUTION OF THE NETWORKS

Within the past five years the simplistic organizational and relational model of these two organizations has changed. In the beginning the function of the regional networks was to create a national bibliographic network.[1] In reviewing the evolution of OCLC especially its structure and activities, the early years seemed to have been characterized by fortunate happenstance more than by strategic planning. OCLC was a rising star which provided an alternative for libraries which appeared very desirable. It was a way for libraries to participate in a national cooperative effort and to begin the creation of a shared bibliographic database. OCLC provided the first realistic efforts to achieve these goals long sought by the profession.

The regional networks have evolved in three primary ways. Some of the regional networks such as BCR had existed for many years as regional cooperative organizations. These groups added another dimension to their activities when they became nodes for OCLC services while still maintaining their original goals and functions. A second group of networks were created solely to provide OCLC services. Examples are MLC or OHIONET. They came into existence solely to provide OCLC services to a geographical grouping of libraries. Some have continued to do only that while others have expanded their mission to include a broader array of activities. The third model is really an OCLC service center such as PACNET.

PACNET was created by OCLC to provide a structure for the western U.S. similar to what existed in the rest of the country since OCLC did not want to deal directly with libraries, and there was no local effort to create a network. With the creation of PACNET in 1976 all states were included in a regional network. Because the origins and the resulting roles of the networks were so different, it was inevitable that the group would never be truly homogeneous.

When the heterogeneity of the regional networks was combined with a changing OCLC, it was only natural that there would be different assessments of roles and functions. By the time the networks were in place, OCLC was going through some dramatic changes. The organization had grown from its initial staff of two serving about 50 Ohio libraries, to a staff of hundreds serving thousands of libraries. When OCLC obtained new leadership in 1981, it took on new dimensions. What had been a loosely structured operation became focused. There was more emphasis on financial viability and future planning than had previously existed. And the organization grew. It was no longer a small, cooperative organization; it was a large corporate structure. At the same time most of the regional networks continued to be relatively modest cooperative activities.

With two disparate types of organizations, there were bound to be differences on how OCLC should interact with the regional networks. And there have been. First was the controversy over the copyright of the online union catalog by OCLC. Then came the continuing network contract dispute. Neither has been completely resolved.

FUTURE RELATIONSHIP FOR OCLC AND THE REGIONAL NETWORKS

This is where the relationship is now. It continues to work but in a somewhat less amicable atmosphere. With this background, what is the future relationship for OCLC and the regional networks? It seems there are several alternatives which might exist.

The first is the status quo. That may sound simple enough, but it is not because the current situation continues to change. As some networks decrease the breadth of their activities others are expanding. Some are maintaining a consistent focus. What this means is that OCLC would have to continue to operate in a heterogenous environment. Each network could be offering a different group of OCLC services causing OCLC to have a multivariate structure to deal with the different levels of services provided by the regional networks. There would continue to be conflicts and disagreements on both sides.

A second alternative would be for OCLC to incorporate the networks into the OCLC structure on the model of PACNET. This would mean the networks would be a part of OCLC, a service center concept. Libraries or general members would still be members of networks, but it would be a different relationship because it would be a relationship with OCLC and not with an organization that they created and controlled. For OCLC, this would provide the type of control they would find most beneficial. There should be no conflicts because all operations would be a part of the same organization. The advantages to OCLC are fairly obvious. Everything is controlled by one organization. All services in a region could be offered through the network. OCLC would be responsible for all costs and there would be a more limited array of services (only OCLC generated services) so it could be less expensive for library members. However, that would not be true if OCLC expanded in any way. On the negative side, the member libraries lose a certain amount of control since the network is an OCLC operation and not a member organization. The existing system of checks and balances would be reduced or eliminated.

A third alternative would be segmentation of the existing networks. In a single purpose network like ILLINET this would not be necessary since it presently has only a single function which is to broker OCLC services. Other networks, however, could segment their activities. OCLC services could be one part; a second segment could be membership/cooperative activities; a third segment could be services which are provided for an additional cost. Or there might be only two parts— OCLC services and everything else. Any more than three segments would be unwieldy to operate. There are many negatives to such a plan:

1. the resulting administrative structure would be cumbersome to operate and administer;
2. it would be difficult to determine in which segment some activities would be included;
3. the overall cost would probably be greater for the organization.

On the plus side, there are several important points:

1. libraries could participate only in those activities in which they were interested;

2. costs to individual libraries might be less since they were only paying for those activities and services in which they wanted to participate;
3. there should be no conflict with OCLC since OCLC services and activities would not be competing with other activities.

The above models are specific to OCLC and the regional networks, but they do also conform to other organizational models which presently exist. Three that are applicable are automobile dealerships, appliance stores, and department stores. Car dealers usually handle one product or a series of products from a single manufacturer. This is the model that would probably be most satisfactory to OCLC. An appliance dealer usually handles appliances from many manufacturers, but it is a single stop for all appliances regardless of the brand. This seems to be the model the networks favor. The department store handles a complete array of products from a variety of suppliers. Neither the regional networks or OCLC would probably like this model, but it would probably serve the best interest of libraries.

Most of what has been discussed has related to the regional networks and OCLC; that was as it should be since that was the topic of this paper. However, there is one part of this equation that has been pushed to the back and that is the libraries or general members. What is it they want and need? It is the libraries that provide OCLC and the regional networks a reason for being. The services provided should be what libraries want or everything has gotten out of perspective. Whom do the networks support? OCLC and the regional networks are making decisions which have a definite impact on libraries. What part are libraries playing in this scenario? Granted there is some input through network boards and OCLC user and advisory groups but are the librarians in these positions representing the needs of the libraries they represent or are they reflecting the needs of the organizations (OCLC or a regional network) they represent in these positions?

For the most part what libraries want is cataloging and interlibrary loan services. As long as these two services are provided the great majority of libraries will be content. However, some libraries have come to expect more. There seem to be two determining factors—size and financial resources. The larger the library, usually the greater the array of services desired, and similarly the more money that is available, the more services the library is likely to require to fulfill its mission.

WHAT IS BEST?

But what is best for the libraries? Omitting the networks to deal directly with OCLC would not seem desirable to many libraries although there are some who do see this as a desirable relationship. Libraries want to work with organizations that they think they know and that understand them. If this assumption is valid, then the networks must continue to exist, and OCLC must accept and encourage that existence. It would appear that most libraries would probably prefer the existing structure or one which segmented services rather than a local OCLC organization.

What is evident is that the networks must continue to evolve just as the environment around them evolves and changes. If they try to remain the same, they will not survive. The networks can continue to adapt to OCLC and its needs by changing internal organization and structure. A second alternative, if one assumes that the networks are needed, is for the networks to become a greater force in influencing OCLC to be more responsive to the libraries' needs and those of the general members. This does not seem to be a strong probability because the networks have not tended to be a cohesive force.

If one looks at the general goals of OCLC and the regional networks, it is apparent that the goals are different but complementary. On the other hand, networks are directed at helping libraries. As the situation evolves, networks will continue to focus on libraries, and OCLC will try to broaden its focus to individual users. There is room for both.

If the networks are to be successful in maintaining their viability there are several factors which will have to be kept in mind. The networks must maintain their membership structure so that libraries feel they are a part of the organization. They must continue to be action-oriented organizations. They must not talk their problems to death or spend inordinate amounts of time trying to create perfect solutions. They need to continue to do what they do best and not stray too far from their areas of expertise. They cannot be all things to all libraries. They must also recognize that service is their most important value. Their autonomy will be important to their future success. And lastly networks will have to find ways to be more effective both internally and externally. If the networks can accomplish these ends, they should be with us for a long time to come.

If OCLC is to continue its rise, there are some similar factors which will have to be heeded. OCLC must continue to do what it does best and that is to provide bibliographic services to libraries. Services to end users will without doubt be one wave of the future which provides a larger potential customer base. However, as libraries expand their roles and missions, the library may maintain its function as the primary provider of information even if it is only the first node in a much larger network. If this happens, services to end users by organizations like OCLC will diminish in importance. To be successful OCLC must maintain a closeness to its users. It must also regain its role as entrepreneur both in terms of services and leadership. Wanting to be first can be a powerful force in an organization. Waiting for someone else to take the risks can leave an organization lagging behind. Just as for the networks, OCLC must be oriented toward implementation which means they must be goal directed.

CONCLUSION

The partnership of OCLC and the networks is one that has served libraries and hence the profession well. The relationship will change, but it must remain. If it does not, it will not only be OCLC and the networks who will lose, but more importantly libraries will lose because there will inevitably be a degradation of service and when libraries lose so do our users. It is time for OCLC and the networks to find a resolution to their differences. There will need to be give and take on the part of both groups so that libraries are the real beneficiaries which is as it should be.

NOTE

1. Kathleen L. Macuszko, *OCLC: A Decade of Development, 1967-1977*. Littleton, Colorado: Libraries Unlimited, 1984. p. 64.

PART II:
THE FUTURE OF NETWORKING

Library Networking: Statement of a Common Vision

Library of Congress
Network Advisory Committee

In May, 1987 two of the major regional bibliographic networks—AMIGOS and SOLINET—held a joint conference. A "Statement of a Common Vision" distributed by the Network Advisory Committee was presented to conference participants for discussion by participants. The statement, which follows, was also presented to the three main conference speakers for reaction. Their papers follow this statement.

A common vision of networking and shared operational objectives is both possible and desirable. However, the diversity among libraries and other information providers and the variety of economic and political factors influencing them is so great as to make impractical a monolithic nationwide network. To promote the concept of "The Nation's Library" as the aggregate of all available information resources and to bind present and future efforts together in principle and philosophy, the Library of Congress Network Advisory Committee recommends the following statement as a common vision of networking:

Our common vision of networking is an environment in which libraries can provide each individual in the United States with equal opportunity of access to resources that will satisfy their and society's information needs and interests. All users should have access on a timely basis to the information they require without being faced with costs beyond their own or society's means.

To realize this vision, there must be technical and intellectual sharing of resources between the public and private sectors; local, state, and federal governments must fulfill their various responsibilities to individuals and society; and the diverse missions of the several types of libraries must be accommodated. As this vision becomes a reality, there will emerge a diverse but coordinated structure of networks rather than a monolithic one. Active research, rapidly developing technology, collaborative leadership, common standards, and shared communications will provide means by which the system will be further shaped as an interlocking series of local, state, regional, national, and international relationships that are capable of serving the nation's information needs.

Toward a Nationwide Library Network

Henriette D. Avram

INTRODUCTION

The topic of this conference is timely—*Managing Resource Sharing: A New Look at Old Beliefs*. Because of advances in technology and setbacks in the economy, we may be at the threshold of a new era in resource sharing, and it should be interesting to reflect on the past in the light of future possibilities and present and future problems. It was suggested that I cover in my presentation—*Toward a Nationwide Library Network*—some of the happenings of the last decade (both successes and failures) and to share with you my concerns as we continue to build the evolving nationwide network. A decade spans the years 1977-1987, but, to include major events, I took the liberty of expanding the period to include 1967-1987.

The issues as I view them are naturally from the perspective of my position at the Library of Congress (LC), but also as an individual deeply involved in resource sharing through networking for many years. In order to put into perspective the magnitude of what has been accomplished in library automation and networking in these past twenty years, let me remind you of the events of 1965-1969. Responding to the interests of the research libraries of the United States, LC accepted the responsibility to implement a distribution service for cataloging data in machine-readable form. And now some mere twenty odd years later we have a library network in place, albeit still evolving, and included as components of it are bibliographic utilities, state and regional networks, state library agency systems, turnkey library systems as well as major custom designed systems for local library

---

Henriette D. Avram is Assistant Librarian for Processing Services at the Library of Congress. Her degrees are from Hunter College and George Washington University. Avram has been a major participant in national library developments and has contributed extensively to numerous library publications. This article was presented at the joint AMIGOS/SOLINET conference in May, 1987.

processing, and the initial phases of computer-to-computer linking to permit access to local as well as remote resources. LC's MARC Distribution Service, the development of the bibliographic utilities and the evolution of other elements of the national bibliographic arena need no further elaboration as to their importance in the present networking scene.

The accomplishments of the past two decades in resource sharing are many in number and noteworthy in substance. A widespread recognition of the importance of standards early on and the cooperation in the formulation and adoption of these standards were basic and provided the foundation for subsequent networking activities. For this remarkable achievement alone, the library community is to be congratulated.

Also of great significance are the several nationwide cooperative retrospective and/or prospective database building projects which are the result of the numerous developments that occurred during the past twenty years. Librarians have a tradition of resource sharing and have worked together in the past at cooperative efforts, but these were so often doomed to failure because of the lack of proper tools. The online-interactive processing capabilities of the bibliographic utilities, where many institutions can search a database and input a record in a timely fashion following the guidelines and the standards of the project, have made it possible to avoid duplicating the efforts of others. We have now clearly demonstrated the proposition that cooperative efforts can be managed successfully with distributed responsibilities.

These projects include CONSER (originally Conversion of Serials and now Cooperative Online Serials), the oldest and perhaps the most successful, established for the purpose of creating a comprehensive database of machine-readable serial records; the CJK (Chinese, Japanese, and Korean) Project, originally begun on the Research Library Information Network (RLIN) and now also underway at OCLC (Online Computer Library Center, Inc., formerly the Ohio College Library Center) for its member institutions; the REMUS (Retrospective Music) project, which is intended to expand the coverage of music materials by creating bibliographic records in machine-readable form; and LC's NACO (originally the Name Authority Cooperative Project and now the National Coordinated Cataloging Operation) project, where forty-one institutions are working with LC to build a nationwide name authority file.

Although our accomplishments have been important as has been our collective participation in library networking during the past decade, it is my opinion that the foundation on which we continue to build could have been firmer. Carol Henderson once described what we have today as a "... diversified, loosely coordinated system of networks."[1] The key word is "loosely" and even here Carol was kind.

In this country, there has always been a fear of the concept of a "locus" of any kind, even for the planning of a nationwide library network, let alone the administration and operation of such a network. As long ago as 1978, the University of Pittsburgh and the National Commission of Libraries and Information Science (NCLIS) co-sponsored a conference in preparation for the first White House Conference entitled, "The Structure and Governance of Library Networking." The words expressed by Bill Welsh in his presentation at this conference bear repeating almost a decade later—"All of these objections must be considered; each of us has a vested interest in seeing a network established with a governance to protect *our* concerns. But let us look at the problems we have encountered, and will continue to encounter, because of the very lack of a national focus, a forum—problems which might have been avoided if such a structure existed. We might be further advanced by now were there a place where policies could be discussed on a national level, input made, consensus reached before individual actions were taken, with oft distressing results. ... Shouldn't we accept the fact that we have challenges which are not being addressed in any coherent systematic fashion?"[2]

A decade later, the same unstructured approach still exists and I submit, as a community, we have suffered from it. As examples, I chose to address what I consider several of the issues of both the past and the present which demonstrate the negative impact of a lack of a nationwide focal point.

NETWORK ADVISORY COMMITTEE

I will digress from a discussion of the issues to describe the activities of the LC Network Advisory Committee (NAC). I believe no group better demonstrates what might have developed into a useful nationwide library network forum, had it been allowed to do so. NAC has an interesting history which is well documented[3] and that history may somewhat be repeating itself, based on the NAC events of the past two years.

The first meeting of what eventually became known as NAC was held in 1976, when LC invited senior representatives from several organizations to discuss the networking issues that were beginning to emerge. What appeared to be developing was a proliferation of networking organizations without any semblance of coordination. The individuals involved determined that it would be useful to continue the discussions. By this time, LC had established a Network Development Office, and the group was invited to serve as an advisory committee to LC for networking. Eleven years later, the committee is still in existence. To the best of my knowledge, there is no other organization like NAC where most segments of the library and information services community are represented (Appendix I lists the present NAC members and their organizations).

NAC's early efforts were concentrated on the preparation of a planning paper which described a library bibliographic component of a national network as the first phase toward the development of a full service network. This component included the development of a communication system and a bibliographic system and provided the facility whereby a member of one utility could access the database and services of another utility. NAC recommended certain tasks be carried out, e.g., the design of a network architecture, the study of a networking organization and management, definition of the roles of the many elements of the library network such as regional networking organizations, state agencies, etc.

The technical aspects for the bibliographic component proceeded with some success. It was this early work that was the basis for the development of the Linked Systems Project (LSP). The study of a networking organization and management, however, went nowhere. In fact, the subcommittee of NAC met for over a year and could never arrive at an agreed upon work statement for contractual support for such a study. And yet, it was recognized by all concerned that the community was in its infancy in this area, and the study would be at best a learning device.

Although the NAC planning paper was discussed at the national library association meetings, made widely available for comments, and public statements were made clearly noting that LC's role was one of coordination and to serve as the secretariat of NAC, it was evident that some very sensitive spots had been touched. There was much criticism directed at NAC and LC for top down versus bottom up planning.

During this same period of time, and based on the efforts of NAC, staffs of the Council on Library Resources (CLR) and the LC Network Development Office prepared a program document which was successfully used by CLR to raise funding for its Bibliographic Service Development Program (including the development of the computer-to-computer link).

In 1979 NAC withdrew from activities of this kind and concentrated its efforts on the identification and further discussion of networking issues and, when applicable, recommendations were made for action to NAC members and other organizations. Interestingly enough, NAC considered itself a discussion forum, as opposed to a planning or coordinating group, during this second (and continuing phase) of its existence. The Committee tackled such topics as ownership and distribution of bibliographic data, network governance, resource sharing, document delivery, emerging statewide computerized bibliographic networks, electronic information delivery systems, public/private sector interactions, and information economy.

Since 1985, however, NAC's deliberations have assumed some of the characteristics of the earlier days. This resulted from a request made to NAC by NCLIS for assistance in revising the networking action of its 1975 program document.[4] In order to do so, NAC devoted a session to the identification of today's key networking issues.

NAC's recommendations following that first session included:

1. NAC should assist NCLIS to develop a strategy to update its program document with a current networking perspective, incorporating NCLIS programs and plans for the proposed 1989 White House Conference;
2. NAC should identify a common vision for networking to coordinate nationwide activities and to guarantee some order in the development of a plan to realize it;
3. NAC should serve as a catalyst to convince the library and information community of the importance of networking; and
4. NAC should urge federal support for networking and library services.

The vision statement precedes this paper. Included in the statement is the sentence, "As this vision becomes a reality, there will emerge a diverse but *coordinated structure* of networks rather than a monolithic one. (The italics are the author's.) The important words are "coordinated structure," as opposed to the expression "loosely coordinated."

Several sessions of NAC were then devoted to an action agenda, i.e., the tasks required to work toward the vision statement. The action agenda consists of twenty-nine tasks, too many to describe here, but, in general, these tasks cluster around the following broad categories: public relations, economic aspects, education on the importance of networking, required research, communications and liaison with other national organizations. Several of these tasks are already underway and contacts having been made with other organizations when required for specific tasks. The vision statement as a whole has been given wide publicity and is under discussion by a number of networking and related organizations.

Barbara Markuson presented an excellent paper to NAC in May, 1985 entitled, *Issues in National Library Network Development: An Overview*. In it, she recognized the role played by NAC, and equally important, she made the following observations:

> I have been frank in identifying key decisions. My intention is not to cast blame; indeed, I was either a participant or an avid onlooker in most of them. My point has been to give us a context for an honest appraisal of where we are now. All of us in this room have collectively labored for hundreds of years for automation, for networking, and for library traditions of open access to information. Each of us starts with a bias toward the institution that we represent. I encourage you to redefine network goals and give us a new vision of what it is possible for us to do. We can begin by looking, not into the future, but into the present. What do we need to do that we can't get done alone? What critical issues are facing our library members and how can we get these addressed? What gains have we made that are of national importance and how can we keep local efforts channeled to support them? How can NAC's deliberations and recommendations help networkers at all levels keep abreast of issues and, where possible, contribute to solutions? How can we, as networkers, work more effectively to deliver better service? What don't we like about what we have become and how can we change? Can we collaborate, accept the strange paths by which we all got here, and get on with it? How do we get the data to the user in Boise still waiting at the terminal?[5]

It appears to me that Markuson is also calling for a focal point. Perhaps NAC could serve as the catalyst to coordinate nationwide efforts?

RETROSPECTIVE CONVERSION

One of the most costly failures of the past has been the lack of a national coordinated effort for retrospective conversion. Since the initial stages of the development of MARC in the late 1960s, there has been the hope that some method could be found to convert the body of previously existing cataloging records into machine-readable form. There were frequent discussions of this topic during the early 1970s, but then the topic lay dormant until the end of the decade. The need for the conversion of these records is now seen as a major concern of national networking in the United States.

Early efforts by LC included the Retrospective Conversion (RECON) Pilot Project beginning in 1969 and the Cooperative MARC Project (COMARC) in the early 1970s. Both these projects were not continued due primarily to a lack of understanding of the importance of retrospective conversion and therefore a lack of support by the library community and, secondarily, to a lack of funding.

The COMARC project closed out the first period of interest in retrospective conversion as a coordinated undertaking. The remaining years of the decade, instead, saw LC increasing the amount of prospective cataloging being entered into MARC and retrospective cataloging being undertaken as required by the needs of individual libraries. This was also the period of the development of large bibliographic utilities and regional networks. Initially, the utilities were mainly used for the creation of records for new cataloging with much less emphasis on retrospective records. The widespread assumption appeared to be, especially among the large research libraries, that the conversion of their complete files of retrospective records was not feasible and that the newly created machine-readable files would augment, not replace, the old card catalogs.

Gradually, as the utilities' databases increased in size through the addition of both LC distributed and member contributed records, some libraries began to realize that a very large proportion of the records needed to convert their retrospective catalogs were in fact in machine-readable form. It was also becoming evident that divided manual/automated catalogs were not efficient for use either by technical processing departments or by reference departments. By the end of the decade, "retrospective conversion" had again become a major topic in library technical processing and automation circles. The utilities began offering retrospective conversion services with, in some cases, full-time staffs devoted to this effort. Service bureaus also appeared that specialized in retrospective conversion.

In 1978, the shelflist of the Library of Congress was microfilmed, and Carrollton Press, Inc. was preparing to produce a title index to it using a machine-readable file derived from the film. The Library entered into an agreement with Carrollton Press whereby it would key additional data elements into the file as it was being created. The Library received copies of these records and loaded them into its online search system, but, because of contractual constraints, was not permitted to distribute them through the MARC Distribution Service.

By the beginning of the 1980s, it was becoming very clear to many individuals that the lack of open access to the ever-increasing store of bibliographic records already converted and the lack of coordination for ongoing retrospective conversion efforts were serious problems for bibliographic control in the United States. In 1983, CLR initiated a study on the status of retrospective conversion in the country. Their report, *Issues in Retrospective Conversion*,[6] gave a thorough overview of the status of retrospective conversion, the issues involved, and a recommendation for a national strategy for retrospective conversion. The discussion of these topics continued with a meeting sponsored by CLR in 1984.[7] In 1985, the Association of Research Libraries (ARL), with support from CLR, undertook a three-month study to develop a proposal for a plan for coordinated retrospective conversion in North America with the goals as follows:[8]

1. Coordinate the systematic conversion of six to seven million yet unconverted monographic records.
2. Make newly converted records accessible through an equitable distribution process.
3. Establish guidelines for records created under the program.
4. Promote active participation by the research library community in the program.
5. Coordinate program projects with existing retrospective conversion efforts.

The strategy proposed was to convert strong research collections with the selection to be based on the subject areas that are of greatest interest to research libraries.

In May 1985, ARL initiated a two-year pilot Recon Project which embraced their stated goals for coordinated retrospective conversion. Recently, at the end of two years of operation, the project was evaluated by ARL's Bibliographic Control Committee. Although the overall results of the project were somewhat mixed, the committee recommended that the project be continued. Also, because of the low success rate in obtaining funding so far in the project, the committee recommended that emphasis be shifted from developing new projects to obtaining funding for projects already planned.

The ARL membership, however, at its May 1987 meeting, saw fit to reduce the program just to a clearinghouse activity—the rationale being that research libraries were competing for funding for other projects with the same funding agencies being approached for RECON projects, and libraries were already engaged in retrospective records individually on their own. I seriously doubt that any other organization will again try to coordinate retrospective conversion activities.

From our current perspective of nearly twenty years of MARC, it does appear that the recommendation of the original RECON Working Task Force for an immediate conversion of retrospective cataloging data should have been followed. It is true that a large number of records for retrospective materials are in machine-readable form, but they are not equally available to all institutions converting their card catalogs. Except for the common element of LC MARC records distributed through the MARC Distribution Service, little is known concerning the duplicate records that may exist. Some records are in the databases of the bibliographic utilities, others in the databases of state or regional networks, and still others in the databases of large or small local systems or independent vendors.

The current problem is not that libraries have not been involved in retrospective conversion or that a large resource of retrospective records does not exist. Instead, the problems seem to be threefold: (1) the lack of sharing of the existing databases of retrospectively converted records, (2) the lack of a rigorous and systematic plan for future conversion efforts, and (3) the lack of clear and rigorous standards for the creation of records for retrospective materials.

It may well be that in the early days of MARC only a few individuals really understood the importance of having our entire retrospective files in machine-readable form. Through the years, however, it has become clear that for all libraries, and especially for large research libraries, the integration of all records in a single catalog is the only efficient means to satisfy the needs of both technical services and reference staffs. For most large libraries, any activities that lie outside the automated procedures and depend on manual catalogs or other files are becoming more and more difficult and expensive to maintain. Complete conversion of our retrospective catalogs has become not so much an *ideal* as a *necessity*. As a community, we have paid the price for the lack of a nationwide coordinated approach for retrospective conversion. The number of duplicate records converted and the aggregate associated costs must be enormous—and this continues.

INTERNATIONAL MARC

My topic, of course, extends beyond a nationwide network. It is, therefore, useful to spend some time describing what has been happening in the international arena and some of the problems that continue to plague us from that perspective. A survey of the current international scene reveals the expansion that has taken place since 1969 when LC launched its MARC Distribution Service. Most national bibliographic agencies have developed similar MARC services, assuming responsibility for the creation of MARC records representing the publishing output of their respective countries. Nineteen countries report the existence of national MARC services; another twenty-five have been identified as being at different stages of planning for a distribution or online service.[9]

Because of the importance given to the exchange of machine-readable records, an International MARC Network Committee was formed in 1975, made up of representatives from those national libraries with MARC programs. The original concept envisioned was that the exchange of MARC data would take place between national libraries, free of charge, for further distribution by the recipient national library to agencies within its country. Although international MARC is flourishing, today the activity is accompanied by a host of problems. It seems that two statements describe the crux of the situation in which we and other countries find ourselves: (1) MARC records have become a commodity; and (2) the altruistic climate which once sustained the national and international exchange of data is eroding. As a result of these developments, a number of issues have surfaced which contribute to the problems now being experienced internationally:

— Organizations other than national libraries are now aggressively seeking MARC data directly from national bibliographic agencies worldwide, often in direct competition with the national agencies in their respective countries. Coupled with this, many national agencies have assumed the role of a bibliographic utility, further intensifying the contention for receiving, processing, and distributing foreign MARC data. Indicative of the growing concern over this particular issue, the Conference of Directors of National Libraries (CDNL) — an affiliate organization to the International Federation of Library Associations and Institutions (IFLA) and parent organization of the International MARC Committee — issued the following two resolutions at its 1986 conference in Tokyo: (1) That national bibliographic agencies agree to inform and consult one another before entering into MARC distribution arrangements with other types of organizations, such as bibliographic utilities, to redistribute MARC records in other countries; and (2) That in cases where a national bibliographic agency finds it advantageous to supply an organization other than a national library in another country with its records for redistribution, that this arrangement not be made exclusive.
— Record ownership has become an issue.
— Restricting the use of records beyond the primary recipient has

been exacerbated by advanced technology which makes possible electronic transmission of data. It becomes virtually impossible to control unauthorized record use.
— National agencies claiming copyright of their data have imposed restrictions on distribution and redistribution of records, both on wholesale and selective bases. Several agencies now only allow wholesale distribution or redistribution when the records have been converted by the recipient national agency as part of its conversion service for converting records to the format of the recipient country, and, even here, additional limitations are often imposed.
— Some national agencies are being forced to increase the price of their services. They bear the entire cost of creating records, while other organizations make money as brokers of the records. Of further concern is the ease of copying MARC records for redistribution, which appreciably reduces the customer base of the national agencies.

PROBLEMS

As agencies move to embrace records from countries whose language, character sets, and cataloging practices and traditions differ dramatically from each other, the ease with which these various records can be accommodated in a machine-readable catalog is considerably diminished. Several problems illustrate the points to be made here:

Problem: *Lack of international cataloging standards*. The International Standard Bibliographic Description (ISBD) has helped significantly with the descriptive aspect of the interchangeability of records, but standardization of choice and form of heading continues to present major obstacles.

Problem: *Lack of international subject control*. In the U.S., *Library of Congress Subject Headings* and LC and Dewey Decimal classification schemes are the classification schemes primarily followed, while in Europe the Universal Decimal classification scheme has more popularity and the British use the PRECIS system. The resulting mixture calls for at least looking into multiple thesauri for the subject headings and seeking ways of handling the different classification schemes.

Problem: *Language barriers*. One of the most obvious differences, namely the different languages used from country to country, can cause the greatest headaches. The language used in the MARC records of a national agency naturally is the language of the country, causing difficulties—especially in subject headings and notes—when records are used by other countries.

Problem: *Non-roman-alphabets*. The acceptance of international romanization schemes by all countries seems remote at best. The complexities of the languages involved are key factors. These complexities are compounded when records prepared by different MARC agencies follow different schemes for romanization, even when the variations are only slight. By the time records from several sources are incorporated into a database, their varying romanized versions will contribute to further discordance.

Of course, it makes a difference whether such records are used only by libraries in the country of origin, where then they will presumably be compatible with other cataloging records in that country.

LC is presently renewing its efforts to make use of foreign MARC data in its processing services. This includes both for its internal applications as well as for conversion for distribution in the U.S. and abroad. Records utilized by LC will be upgraded to reflect its cataloging practices and distributed as an LC MARC record. If this upgrade is too labor intensive, it may prove more cost effective for LC to do original cataloging and conversion.

A market survey has been prepared and is about to be sent to customers of LC's Cataloging Distribution Service to determine what interest there may be for a distribution service for each foreign MARC tape service. The results will aid LC in developing any services deemed beneficial for distribution.

During the past year or so, LC has been actively pursuing a means to make use of Japanese MARC records produced by the National Diet Library. The major task required here has been to reconcile the differences in the cataloging rules used, differences in character representations, and differences in the romanization schemes employed. Successful completion of this investigation will enable LC to distribute such converted records to RLIN and OCLC to support their CJK Projects.

LC is also re-examining its exchange agreements with other national libraries. As part of this re-examination, it will look at implementing licensing agreements without seriously impacting those it is committed to helping, e.g., other national agencies and LC's smaller customers. The coming year is likely to produce new arrangements from LC for selective and wholesale distribution and redistribution of its records.

LC has a continuing commitment to work toward building files which can be truly useful in the years to come, as more and more foreign data from many sources are added to our databases. Here again, a forum for the coordination as to planning and implementation for the use of foreign MARC data would be most useful to all concerned.

COPYRIGHT ISSUES

Consideration of the protection of intellectual property rights in this age of rapidly advancing technology is one of the most complex issues facing society today. Networking databases contain either bibliographic records that are in the public domain or that are protected by copyright law. Under the copyright law, databases are categorized as compilations; compilations in this context are defined as works resulting from the selection, coordination and arrangement of preexisting materials.

Copyright given to the entire compilation extends only to the material added by a human author. That means in the case of the entire compilation of a bibliographic database, the material added by human authors are the records from one or more libraries. The organization that compiles the database may also contribute copyrightable authorship, because they may also be "massaging" the data that makes up the compilation. Copyright of any underlying work in the compilation is not affected by the copyright in the compilation (e.g., if a library owns the copyrighting of its records, it still retains those rights even though the records have become part of a larger compilation which may also be copyrightable).

To be copyrightable, the work must be *original*; that is, there must be a certain minimum amount of selection, coordination or arrangement. Thus, not all compilations are copyrightable.

In the library community, until the recent past, most resource sharing databases have contained bibliographic records and not traditional copyrightable works such as printed materials in machine-readable form. Rights and use have generally been determined by contract; copyright law has not been very important. However, as loss of control over end users becomes more real, and as libraries put traditional works in digital form for storage and access purposes (e.g., the Library of Congress' optical disk program), copyright becomes more central.

With regard to traditional works (e.g., a journal, a musical composition, a photograph), permission of the owner of the right of reproduction would be required to input such a work into a computer system. If the work is to be viewed on a computer terminal, the right to publicly display the work is also required. General principles of copyright law apply, including fair use.

With regard to historical, medical, scientific, census, military, financial, and personnel fact-based databases and also bibliographic databases, the issues are more difficult. Courts in the United States have handled such compilations in a confusing manner. Some courts apply traditional copyright tests when deciding whether or not the database is original. These courts look for the exercise of judgment or individual creativity. Thus, it was held that selecting 5,000 premier baseball cards out of a possible 17,000 and publishing the compilation in a guide was protectable authorship (*Eckes v. Card Price Update*, 736 F. 2d 859 [2d Cir. 1984]). However, in a case involving form cards, which were filled out and provided information on municipal bonds, the court found that the compilation of data was not copyrightable. The information was factual and only certain information was reported. The court noted that the individual data elements were selected to conform to a predetermined uniform format and there had been no individual selection, choice or judgment (*Financial Information Inc. v. Moody's Investment Service, Inc.*, 808 F. 2d 204 [2d Cir. 1986]).

Other courts have consistently protected the labor involved in producing a compilation, called "sweat of the brow" authorship. In these cases the courts are protecting the expense, time and effort that went into producing the work. For example, recently it was held that the West Publishing Company's pagination of court decisions which are in the public domain was protected because of West's selection of the *order* in which it assembles the cases for publication (*West Publishing Co. v. Mead Data Central, Inc.*, 799 1219 [8th Cir. 1986]).

The problem with many bibliographic databases is that the selection and ordering of the bibliographic entries is often predetermined and the effort is to make the database totally comprehensive (i.e., the goal is to put in as many records as possible). The question is—does the effort in creating such databases result in a copyrightable work? Also, are individual bibliographic records original and therefore copyrightable? The answer in the United States today is maybe yes, maybe no. This is because the basis for copyright protection in such works is presently unclear.

Assuming that the database or the individual bibliographic entry is copyrightable, another question is who owns the literary property rights? What rights are there, and what constitutes an infringement? Of course, if there is a contract, the contract determines the answers to these questions as far as the parties to the contract are concerned.

The copyright in the individual bibliographic records would belong to the author, in this case the library. Also, as a copyright owner, the organization that collects, assembles and disseminates the database has the right to control reproduction and public display of the compilation. A work is infringed when one or more of the rights accorded to the copyright owner are violated. With regard to the reproduction rights, this means that a copyrighted compilation of one or more library's contribution to the compilation would be infringed by reproducing it in whole or in any substantial part, and by duplicating it exactly. What is "substantial" is a question of fact which is resolved by courts on a case by case basis.

Traditional works and factual databases as well as bibliographic databases will be part of the network of the future. How to provide legal protection that is most suitable to network use is not totally clear. Allocation of royalties to the appropriate parties may be necessary. It would seem that new legal structures will be required.

NAC's most recent meeting held in April, 1987 was focused on a review of the Congressional Office of Technology Assessment's (OTA) report, *Intellectual Property Rights in an Age of Electronics and Information*. The invited speakers included Linda Garcia and Robert Kost from the OTA study; Ralph Oman, Register of Copyrights; Michael Remington, Chief Counsel to the House copyright subcommittee; David Laird, University of Arizona Libraries; Barbara Polansky and John Hearty from the American Chemical Society, and David Peyton, Information Industry Association.

It was clear from the presentations and the discussions following that many of the issues are of vital interest to libraries, in particular, because of their participation in networking. Mr. Remington noted that the House copyright subcommittee would be interested in learning of the special needs of libraries from an organization such as NAC. NAC members agreed that the fall, 1987 meeting should be devoted to this topic.

Perhaps the possibility exists that some of the major issues affecting libraries and networks concerning intellectual property rights can be identified by NAC, discussed by the constituents of NAC representatives, and those issues agreed upon by the community as critical forwarded by NAC for attention to the House copyright subcommittee. Here NAC would serve as a focal point.

LINKED SYSTEMS PROJECT

The Linked Systems Project (LSP) began formally in 1980 with funding from CLR. Initially, there were three participants, LC, the Research Libraries Group (RLG), and the Western Library Network (WLN) — formerly the Washington Library Network, with OCLC joining later as a fourth participant. The activity was conceived in order to provide a solution to the problem that the members of one bibliographic utility could only share resources with other members of the same utility but had no access to data on the other utilities. Thus, there still remained costly duplicate cataloging and conversion.

The challenge was to build a nationwide linking system made up of four independent systems, each with its own tailor-made system architecture, which could operate with the efficiencies of a single network and increase national resource sharing. Later in the life of the project, the decreasing cost of hardware with the availability of mini and micro computers (as well as less expensive mainframes) and the increasing cost of telecommunications led to the growing popularity of regional and local systems. Thus, the concept of a linked nationwide library network was expanded to include, for example, connecting local systems in a region, local systems in a single institution, local systems to utilities and vice versa.

Since authority work is the single most expensive aspect of the cataloging process and is critical to the maintenance of a consistent catalog, and since the LC NACO project was already underway, authority data exchange was the first application to be implemented under LSP. NACO libraries, through their utilities, will contribute records to LC. These records will be incorporated into LC's machine-readable catalogs and distributed via the link to the other LSP participants, along with records created by LC. Likewise, all records will be made available through the regular MARC Distribution Service.

The status of the authorities implementation is that LC distributes approximately 2,500 authority records to RLIN and OCLC daily over the link. Therefore, all users of the two utilities have available an exact duplicate (minus twenty-four hours) of LC's authority file including "early notice records." (Early notice records are preliminary records noting work is underway and have never been made available outside of LC before). The contribution of records to LC by NACO members is now operational at RLIN, and the first NACO participant will be Yale University; at OCLC, the contribution process is fully underway, the benefits to LC will also be substantial. NACO records no longer will be keyed by LC and thus will be available for use by all faster.

Since the present authority application is an augmentation of the NACO project, the exchange of data is between LC and each utility only. The system is so designed, however, that the facility to transfer records and perform intersystem searching can be extended to operate between any two systems desiring to communicate, e.g., the utilities, with each other. The tremendous advantage of LSP is that for both the input of records and for intersystem searching, the user employs the terminal, the familiar procedures, and the query languages of his local system. Responses made to the user at his terminal, regardless of the system in which the record was originally housed, are displayed in the format of his system.

In effect then, for searching, the user has a direct connection to the remote system through his own system. If the user instead had to dial the remote system directly, the input of the record and the search query would be formulated according to the conventions of that system, the results would be displayed in an unfamiliar format, and a different terminal most likely would be required. By using computer-to-computer communication instead, the user offloads to the computer the burden of resolving these differences. Equally as important, by transferring records from computer to computer rather than from computer to terminal, as a result of a search the user now has immediate access to the records in machine-readable form, so they can be modified and added to the local databases.

The next LSP application, already in the design stage, will be the transmission of cataloging records. Initially, it is planned that this capability will be used to support a major coordinated undertaking between LC and a selected group of research libraries. The group of libraries will contribute cataloging and authority records to LC via their utilities, following LC's cataloging practices and procedures. The resulting records, as part of LC's catalog, will be maintained by LC. LC will also make the original and corrected records available via the link and its regular MARC Distribution Service. The result of this activity is the building of a consistent national database, where the access points on each bibliographic record are established in accordance with a verified authority record.

What else can we do with LSP? LSP will provide the capability to do many operations that we presently cannot do. For example, CONSER records are housed on OCLC. Several CONSER members are members of RLIN and have no mechanism (1) to search the CONSER file on OCLC to determine if a record already exists or (2) to input an original record to the RLIN system which in turn will be transmitted to OCLC so that a CONSER member of OCLC will not duplicate cataloging and conversion. Tape exchange is far too slow to be effective. LSP would greatly enhance CONSER and, in fact, any cooperative prospective or retrospective cooperative project where the cooperating parties are using different systems.

LSP is already being used to link local systems to a utility. A link is operational between RLIN and New York University for the transmission of bibliographic records, and work is underway at Northwestern University to link the NOTIS system to RLIN. LSP will provide the mechanism to download records between utility and local system and to upload records between local system and utility, thus preserving the resource sharing capabilities we have worked so hard to accomplish and at the same time allow libraries to carry out certain functions which are better performed locally.

A key technical decision made by the LSP participants was to base the system on the International Organization of Standardization (ISO) Open Systems Interconnection (OSI) Reference Manual. These protocols have been and are being adopted by consensus, in the open arena of the standards world rather than being designed for a single manufacturer or type of activity.

With all these wonderful things happening, what are the problems? Someone said recently that the library community needed LSP yesterday. Little did that person realize that LSP had its genesis in 1976 under the auspices of NAC, was underway in 1980, and here it is 1987 — not great progress — why? The technology required for LSP is available. The bibliographic problems, albeit difficult, are solvable. The political and economic issues sometimes seem insurmountable and account for the long development time. Database ownership — how do you restrict the use in a linking system? How do you guarantee economic viability for those organizations dependent on income from a database asset? These and other questions have caused a "dragging of the feet."

LSP could have been implemented in a much shorter time frame, again putting librarians out in the forefront of technology, but this was not to be the case. The implementation of LSP was dependent on several organizations, and there was no mechanism to accelerate any individual organization development. Nor did there exist a forum to discuss the pros and cons of LSP and investigate possible solutions to the political and economic problems.

How each organization will participate in LSP will be determined by that organization. Many factors will come into play such as the traffic flow that unrestricted searching could create, databases which have limitations imposed on their availability, and the imbalance existing between the number of members of one utility versus the number of members on another utility when intersystem searching and record transfer is employed.

The LSP Policy Committee, made up of senior officers of RLG, OCLC, and LC, and a member of RLAC (The Research Libraries

Advisory Committee to OCLC), was established in 1985 to address these and other policy matters.

Although the paper written by James Rice was not yet published at this presentation in New Orleans, I was aware of its existence. Since it so well represents my feelings, I have taken the liberty of quoting here:

> To sum up, the evolution of the open system approach will be much like the evolution of the MARC communications format in many ways: It will develop slowly; many vendors and other product designers will not recognize its importance until they have made mistakes that could have been avoided; it will be an internationally adopted set of standards; and it will enable certain types of library automation to exist that could never have been possible otherwise. As with MARC, what seems so difficult, so costly, and so rigid is in the long run easier, less expensive, and more flexible. The adoption of the OSI architecture by the Linked Systems Project will go down in history as one of the most important developments in this profession.[10]

CONCLUSION

My attempt today has been to share with you my concern that there does not exist any effective vehicle for national planning and coordination. Consequently, our time and energies are ofttimes wasted mending fences, justifying decisions, and a myriad of tasks—mostly not directed toward the accomplishment of any useful goal.

It appears encouraging that there will be another White House Conference in the 1989-1991 time frame. We now have twenty years experience to consider in our deliberations and perhaps resulting from the conference will come direction for future planning and development in a more orderly fashion.

NOTES

1. "Networks and Public Policy," prepared as a background paper for the July, 1986 Network Advisory Committee meeting, held in Washington, D.C. and to be published in: *Network Planning Paper*, No. 15, 1987.

2. Allen Kent and Thomas J. Galvin, eds. *The Structure and Governance of Library Networks*. (New York: Marcel Dekker, 1979), p. 276.

3. "The Library of Congress Network Advisory Committee: Its First Decade," prepared by Lenore S. Maruyama. *Network-Planning Paper*. no. 11. (Washington, D.C.: Library of Congress, 1985.)

4. *Toward a National Program for Library and Information Services: Goals for Action.* (Washington, D.C.: National Commission on Libraries and Information Science, 1975.)

5. "Key Issues in the Networking Field Today: Proceedings of the Library of Congress Network Advisory Committee Meeting, May 6-8, 1985." *Network Planning Paper*, no. 12. (Washington, D.C.: Library of Congress, 1985), p. 31.

6. Jutta Reed-Scott, Dorothy Gregory, and Charles Payne. *Issues in Retrospective Conversion: Report of a Study Conducted for the Council on Library Resources.* (Washington, D.C.: Council on Library Resources, 1984.)

7. Dorothy Gregor, ed. *Retrospective Conversion: Report of a Meeting Sponsored by the Council on Library Resources, July 16- 18, 1984.* (Washington, D.C.: Council on Library Resources, 1984.)

8. Jutta Reed-Scott. *Plan for a North American Program for Coordinated Retrospective Conversion: Report of a Study Conducted by the Association of Research Libraries.* (Washington, D.C.: Association of Research Libraries, 1985), p. 29.

9. *International Guide to MARC Databases and Services.* 2nd rev. ed. (Frankfurt am Main: International MARC Project, Deutsche Bibliothek, 1986.)

10. James Rice, "Open Systems: a Second Opinion," *American Libraries.* 18 (June, 1987), p. 453.

APPENDIX I

LIBRARY OF CONGRESS
NETWORK ADVISORY COMMITTEE MEMBERS

Akeroyd, Richard, Chief Officers of State Library Agencies

Andre, Pamela Q., National Agricultural Library

Arterbery, Vivian J., National Commission on Libraries and Information Science

Asleson, Robert, Information Industry Association

Avram, Henriette D., Chair, Library of Congress

Bourne, Charles, DIALOG Information Services, Inc.

Broadbent, H.E., III, Pittsburgh Regional Library Center

Brunell, David H., Bibliographical Center for Research

Buckland, Michael K., University of California

Colaianni, Lois Ann, National Library of Medicine

DeJohn, William, Minnesota Interlibrary Telecommunications Exchange

Dillehay, Bette H., Special Libraries Association

Evans, Max J., Society of American Archivists

Grisham, Frank P., Southeastern Library Network

Henderson, Carol C., American Library Association

Jacob, Mary Ellen, OCLC, Inc.

Love, Erika, Medical Library Association

Messmore, Ann B., National Federation of Abstracting and Information Services

Miller, Ronald F., Cooperative Library Agency for Systems and Services

Mockus, Laima, NELINET, Inc.

Oakley, Robert L., American Association of Law Libraries

Paul, Sandra K., Association of American Publishers

Payne, Charles T., University of Chicago

Shaw, Ward, American Society for Information Science

Riley, James P., Federal Library and Information Center Committee

Schmidt, C. James, Research Libraries Group, Inc.

Shubert, Joseph F., American Library Association

APPENDIX I, continued

Studer, William J., Association of Research Libraries
Stussy, Norris A., Western Library Network
Velazquez, Harriet, Utlas International Canada
Wetherbee, Louella V., AMIGOS Bibliographic Council

Strategies for Networking in the Next Ten Years

D. Kaye Gapen

TWO QUESTIONS

In looking at libraries of any type, there are two questions to be considered in assessing the value of what is accomplished. First, where does the library allocate the available energy, time, materials, labor and money? The second question asks what kinds of activities the library performs with its allocations. It should be kept in mind that the basic consideration behind these questions is what the library does to facilitate choice by its users.

CHANGE IN MEANING OF PHYSICAL ACCESS

All types of libraries perform similar basic enhancing activities. Probably the most important value added by libraries of all types is "physical access" to an organized collection of materials. It is of interest to note here, that there has been a gradual change in the meaning of physical access. Sixty years ago, it meant access to a collection of books in a single location called a library. On occasion and by prior agreement an item might be lent by one institution to another for use by a patron of the latter institution. With the gradual realization that no single library, academic or otherwise, could afford to acquire and store all the materials needed by its publics, local union catalogs, the National Union Catalog, the Union List of Serials, and computerized union catalogs such as OCLC were developed. These were means of providing a central record of the holdings of a group of cooperating libraries. In the beginning, access among the institutions in these networks was entirely by mail. Telephone, teletype, and now the com-

---

D. Kaye Gapen earned a BA in Sociology and an MLS from the University of Washington. She is currently Director, General Library System of the University of Wisconsin. Gapen is a member of the OCLC Board. This paper was presented at the joint AMIGOS/SOLINET meeting in May, 1987.

puter and associated telecommunications technologies provide quick, quantitative data anywhere in the country, or the world. Thus the activities of providing physical access have in the past 30 years changed markedly. The potential for continuing and even more rapid change is quite high.

So, one reason that the library world eventually created something like OCLC was to try to provide more scholarship, knowledge, and leisure reading through sharing resources. The second reason that we eventually created CCLC and RLIN is that libraries cost a lot of money to establish and maintain.

All libraries—though some more than others—are labor-intensive operations, both physically and intellectually. Handling thousands, or tens of thousands, or hundreds of thousands, or millions of volumes each year requires people; keeping libraries open requires people; providing reference and information mediation services in support of teaching and scholarship requires people. Electronic publishing formats require even more professional/intellectual mediation and, thus, more people. And, importantly, the changing nature of information and publishing requires new sets of skills that must complement the skills and intellectual abilities necessary to maintain information access as we know it today. This is one of the primary reasons that "access" costs are as important as "collection" costs.

COSTS

In order to make books and journals available it is necessary to undertake a series of processing steps which are labor-intensive and, although productivity has been increased by the use of computers, there is still a linear increase in access costs for each added acquisitions dollar. My estimate is that for every dollar spent on books, $.70-$1.50 is needed to prepare the book for the shelf and get cards into the public catalog.

In 1973, two economists, Baumol and Marcus, wrote in relation to the economics of libraries, that the quantity of labor involved per unit is fixed by the nature of the products, and the quality of the end product is directly dependent on the amount of labor expended per unit of production. Libraries offer services that require personal attention and depend primarily on the amount of human effort devoted to them. Increasing productivity in such an environment is extremely difficult, although the benefits of computerization can have significant impact, depending upon the type of implementation. But electronic systems in libraries have proceeded far less rapidly than their benefit would indicate. A major impediment to change in library operations is the start-up costs of software, computer equipment, and operational costs. Baumol and Marcus suggested that the cost trends resulting from labor-intensive library operation, despite the increased use of computerization, would persist for two decades.

We are now at the end of the first of the two decades posited by Baumol and Marcus. We have begun to see some changes in library information access cost trends, particularly from our extended experience with OCLC as a shared cataloging resource. Automation still remains a logical approach to improving library services while seeking cost control.

It is important to note that we entered into cooperative and networking activities to (1) improve access to resources through sharing and (2) try and increase productivity and control the rate of rise of per unit library costs. It is also important to note that the balance may shift between the two, but that both continue to exist as important and mutually exclusive goals.

THE SYNERGY OF SHARING

Now what does all of this have to do with Henriette Avram's paper? Much of what Henriette talked about seems far removed from our reality of today—indeed, I lived through a great deal of what Henriette described, and it seems far removed from today's reality. But the fact is that we would not be where we are today had it not been for the creation and application of the MARC Format, AACR2, etc. But where did the synergy come from for the creation of these powerful tools—from Oshkosh Public Library, from the small private Alabama academic library? Only very indirectly by the representation of those libraries in the ALA representation which participated in the conceptualization and creation of MARC et al.

Indeed, when these tools were being conceptualized, networks as we know them today did not exist. There was networking going on supported by union card catalogs, but networks as we know them (and have seen them come and go) came about as a result of OCLC. Do you remember that Fred Kilgour said "in order to participate, you have to network?"

In any case, those very powerful tools were created, by and large, by representatives of large and medium sized libraries—either directly or through professional organizations. Even today, it seems as though they continue to exist more for those libraries—Henriette's discussion of international record sharing and the ARL retrospective conversion activities. But they have meant a heck of a lot to all of us because they enabled us to pool our money and create OCLC—and through that creation we have all met our two mutually exclusive goals—resource-sharing and increased productivity. And, in the process, we have learned a great deal about the synergy of sharing.

For, in the course of building OCLC, we also built our local networks, and as we were doing all of this building and defining, the social and economic environment continued to change around us. Manfred Kochen attributes the secret of synergy to the network, and all of us as librarians have found, I believe, synergy levels changing as our networking has matured, grown, or as we have created new networks. Today, our networking gestalt is all at the same time troubled, hopeful, cynical, and frustrated.

EMBRACERS OF ERROR

A good philosophical stance is that:

> There is no need to expect that with the application of knowledge and skill things should always turn out right. Instead there is a growing recognition that it is necessary and responsible to arrange all human and organization resources so that they are future-responsive, so that they act in the present out of a concern for the future. The task is to enlarge our awareness of what is happening and what might happen. This means becoming learners as persons and organizations. It means learning how to become learners and to be learners we must become embracers of error.[1]

The worst thing that could be said of us today is that we are sincere, but still stupid. When our networking and resource-sharing has worked best it has worked because we acted with a healthy view of relationships. We can look at all of the "cool" models that are available and think of applying them. But we have also remembered that our cool models exist hand in hand with hot cognitions. Most models call for rational scanning of alternatives and the calculation of probably gains and losses—i.e., cool models. But hot cognitions result in limitations stemming from imperfect information, human impatience, and the difficulty of adding into our equations the emotional components of hope and fear, not to mention our unconscious projections and fantasies. There is no final resolution of our hot cognitions (for which we should probably be thankful), but it is important that they be right out there in the front as we assess our various models.

So, it is important to begin discussion about changes and progress with what you and I think about what a man or woman is and how she or he works. Because, whether or not we talk about what we think about people clearly, we have formed for ourselves expectations about how others behave toward us and/or will respond to something we do.

My model of human has been and is one which is being discussed in present behavioral science studies as the open system model of man. There is no one proponent or hypothesis for this particular concept, but the major thrust of such a model is the transactional nature of people—rather than being passive agents reacting to stimuli, people are viewed as active and proactive agents, purposive in nature and problem-solving organisms. Also in this model, each individual selectively perceives and interprets the influences of environment and the configuration of different factors and forces. Needless to say, this is not the model that is traditionally characteristic of the industrial age and its hierarchical organizations.

It is the model which is characteristic of networking—where everybody worked out how everybody got a little bit through the sharing—and the whole received something which they would never have received had they remained alone. Because we are not only talking about the benefits of improving access to collections, and lowering the rate of rise of per unit costs—we are talking about what happens when minds and personalities come together to try and solve many different societal problems at the same time. It is then that we realize that none of us is an island, and our local problems or our specialty problems cannot be viewed alone. Indeed, there is creativity and energy to be found in posing and solving problems together.

DUALITIES IN ORDER TO EMBRACE ERROR

And, I hope it is then, that we remember to bring our attention to the long-term and the short-term. I believe that is the combined approach which we *must* take into the '90s and beyond 2000. I have some dualities which I don't want forgotten:

- the duality of resource-sharing and productivity increases
- the duality of short-term and long-term
- the duality of document-based collections and electronic-based collections

I want to put forward the idea that the computerization of library activities to date has not really been anything but the application of a new tool. Computerization alone has not required us to develop a new framework of thought or a scheme for understanding and explaining a new reality. Library computerization has not required a new "paradigm" — a new way of thinking about old problems. With library computerization today, we are still saying as said the king in a *New Yorker* cartoon: "I *can so* repair Humpty Dumpty — but I need more horses and more men."

We are in danger of trying to solve tomorrow's problems with yesterday's tools — those tools being computerization, MARC, AACR2, yesterday's networking. And I apply this to every size of library and to every type of library.

NEW PARADIGM

Now we aren't blind, and many people have been thinking about and searching for a possible new context and for the key that would unlock our vision of the logic of a new paradigm. I suggest to you that the new thing on our horizon, "the key," is electronic information. It requires of us a new paradigm, not because it is new, but because it has some essential characteristics with which we must deal and which are different from anything we have dealt with up to this point. The fact is that our present collections, which are in paper, microformats, tapes, sound recordings, maps, AV materials, etc. are in "handleable" form and can be delivered to the patron physically (i.e., in analog form). We have achieved an impressive degree of integration of these physical formats in almost all of our library operations. For example, we have integrated theogical bibliographic access to these forms by and large in one card catalog, these physical formats physically in our various collections with appropriate guides and self-help finding tools, these physical formats in our centrally funded budgets, and we provide all of them to the library user community at no charge.

Electronic information, however, is created in digital form, is stored digitally on a variety of computer disc devices, and can be delivered digitally over a variety of telecommunications/telephonic networks. Electronic information is an increasing influence in manuscript preparation and book production in the publishing world. It is increasingly important in research, where calculating and computing are integral to the research. It is becoming extraordinarily useful in any work having to do with graphics. It is often available in addition to the physical volume. It is now as often as not the primary or only source of the information (i.e., taking the place of hardcopy formats). And, for government information, it is becoming an increasingly present format.

Electronic/telecommunications networks over which this electronic information can be transmitted and shared are proliferating on campuses and throughout states across the nation, and as we consider the integration of electronic information with our present collections, we face a host of questions and a major challenge: (1) how can we integrate electronic information physically with the present collections so that it is clear to all that both forms of information are available? (2) how can we logically integrate the bibliographic access we currently provide with all of the online secondary literature which provide access to electronic information? (3) how can we adjust our collection development policies and budgets to provide access to electronic primary literature? (4) how can we adjust our information distribution patterns in order to incorporate the distribution of electronic information? These are the first and the easiest questions, and they revolve around the basic functions that we undertake: acquisitions of resources, creation of entry points, mediation of retrieval and delivery of the resources.

A harder, and more interesting question, is how we adapt our resource-sharing mechanisms to include electronic information — and in that integration, how do we continue to try to meet our dual goals of resource-sharing to increase physical access, and resource-sharing to help control costs? A second and more troubling set of questions is part of the environment of our present research library world, in which we rely to a greater and greater extent on computers to provide a higher level of information service, one that adds high level information manipulation and synthesis to a larger and larger degree.

A second major element of the new paradigm involves communication channels. It has recently been stated in the *EDUCOM Bulletin* that:

> Scientific research has always relied on communication for gathering and providing access to data; for exchanging information; for holding discussions, meetings, and seminars; for collaborating with widely dispersed researchers and for disseminating results. The pace and complexity of modern research, especially collaborations of researchers in different institutions, has dramatically increased scientists' communications needs. Scientists now need immediate access to data and information to colleagues and collaborators, and to advanced computing and information

services. Furthermore, to be really useful, communication facilities must be integrated with the scientist's normal day-to-day working environment. Scientists depend on computing and communications tools and are handicapped without them . . . computer networks provide the base that combines geographically dispersed researchers, computing resources, and information into a single integrated computer and communications environment.[2]

Scientists, in the end, are no different from other people who want to learn, teach, and do scholarship. What we see in their use patterns today is what we are likely to see in other use patterns tomorrow. I believe, then, that scientists and other citizens are beginning to be able to view libraries of any kind as information systems — and information systems which are more than question-answering systems. Our libraries now are becoming information systems which address problems, which clarify problems, and which attack problems. Any human intermediary — cataloger, selector, reference person, shelver — searcher, analyst, evaluator, synthesizer, or interpreter — is part of the information system. By concentrating on the true end-user of an information system and on the ultimate use of the information, we place emphasis on the real functions and purposes of the information system.

RESOURCE-SHARING ASSUMPTIONS

I believe that evolving patterns associated with electronic information will have a significant impact on the resource sharing role of all libraries in the provision of local information services, statewide information services, regional information services, national information services, and international information services:

1. Libraries and knowledge are labor intensive. For every dollar we spend on getting a book, we are all spending from 75 cents to $1.50 to make that book accessible. Any decisions must relate to this labor intensity.
2. Technology impacts society, education, scholarship, and libraries and scholarly communication patterns, electronic information, new kinds of formal and informal networking.
3. Electronic information is creating a new paradigm for universities and libraries which must be integrated with our present paradigm which is based on maintaining a useable inventory of physical pieces — volumes — books.

4. We are, thus, bimodal. In one mode of service we provide document-based collection resources in response to teaching and research programs. In a second mode of service we provide access to electronic information in response to teaching and research programs. The methods of providing access to these two modes are very different and all of us are only at the very early stage of integrating the two modes into a unified whole—a whole and integrated organizational approach, and a whole and integrated professional approach for us as individuals.
5. Paramount in these considerations is that we are "close" to the information problems which the members of our communities have. We want to be able to design our library services to meet the specific needs of a person in a particular environment with a particular problem. This implies knowledge of that person's style, bias, idiosyncracies, and sophistication, as well as the politics and constraints of the context.
6. There is a clear implication, too, that the librarian is also becoming a "technologist"—i.e., one cannot access the information without understanding and working a variety of technologies. There is a clear and complex interrelationship between the information and the equipment—with as many relationships as there are sets of hardware and software.
7. This indicates a key difference between a document-based information system and an electronic information system in which there is a dichotomy of approach—the document-based system is a container—the electronic information system is a communication process. (A note about CD-ROM products—in this context I consider them a container—they become part of a communication process only when they can be transmitted/delivered electronically.)
8. Libraries, then, are including as part of their resources:
STAFF: who now become as important a resource as the collection
DOCUMENT-BASED COLLECTIONS: our libraries as we know them by and large today.
ELECTRONIC INFORMATION: in packages such as CD ROM products.
GATEWAYS: including access to data and information outside the library, access to data and information inside the library, telecommunications networks outside the local area, and telecommunications networks inside the local area. (By "data" and "information" I mean primary and secondary literatures.)

EVELYN DANIELS

Evelyn Daniels has said that the university library (and I would say all libraries) are connected in sophisticated and symbiotic ways to national cataloging utilities, to national policy-making groups and to other individual libraries in a variety of simple-to-complex relationships. It would be hard to identify any other institution that had achieved the network of cooperative relationships that university libraries have developed over the years. Although the mainframe library is still an important fixture on each campus and will probably continue to be for a long time to come, it also can be viewed as a switching center connecting users to materials from all over the world. Online catalogs allow increasingly transparent bibliographic access to the world's documentary sources via telephone links to the library's computers while physical delivery lags.

This changing interlinked system has been costly to create economically and is also proving costly in psychological ways for librarians who were educated for one kind of technology and who have had to retrain on the job in order to comprehend a very different kind of technology that has brought with it considerably more complicated organizational forms. Further changes will be required in order to realize the dream of universal subject access to all documentary sources of information in a way that transcends the container, the language, and the location.

STRATEGIES FOR NETWORKING

Manfred Kochen compares the networking functions in the human brain to the networking functions in the social, scientific community. Communication is the vital ingredient and the network is the synergy generator.

1. So, my first strategy is to maintain my network relationships as energy generators for some time into the future. I need this synergy because I have to ask myself new questions—I don't want to answer yesterday's questions, I want to answer tomorrow's questions.
2. Within my various networking relationships I want to use the synergy of the network to explore new scenarios of resource-sharing. I have explored the evolving patterns associated with government information in electronic format and have said the following:

a. Because of the breadth and depth of their collections, research libraries tend to serve as resource collections for other libraries. As more multitype libraries have used OCLC or RLIN for retroactive and current cataloging, the presence of their holdings has spread interlibrary loan requests among a larger number of libraries, although the general pattern of research libraries as net lenders seems to be continuing.

b. Resource sharing among depository libraries will change as electronic products are added and become critical sources of information. It is possible that different types of libraries will define new scopes for their depository collections and offer a more focused but well-defined array of services for the collection.

c. Depositories will probably become more differentiated than they are today with research libraries playing a more substantial role because they have sufficient funding and staffing to provide some flexibility in responding and adapting to these changing patterns. All libraries, however, will continue to accept the mission of making information available to the public.

d. There will be new choices to be made in smaller libraries between low fixed costs and high incremental costs per search strategy. Larger libraries are more likely to choose the high fixed cost and low incremental cost strategy at least for very commonly used datafiles. They may be in a position to provide access to other depository libraries with cost recovery from some source.

e. With the incorporation of electronic products, it should be recognized that different depository libraries can take advantage of different kinds of products to different degrees. It may be to the advantage of the Depository Library Program if, for some electronic materials, a few large libraries serve as intermediaries for all other depositories as well as for remote users of information. Moreover, strengthening existing and defining new relationships among all libraries will be desirable.

We could easily have in our new resource sharing patterns the following framework, within which networking for resource sharing and cost control take on whole new patterns.

Basic Services: This level would serve as an information center in which there would exist a small collection of documents and a computerized gateway to electronic government information located elsewhere. The service might be focused more on self-help and on-demand levels. There would be a high cost per transaction but a small fixed cost.

Intermediate: This level of library would maintain a larger government document-based collection and some electronic information and gateways to other electronic information located elsewhere. This library might devise products which would work well through the gateways and might invest in developing value-added approaches to the information. The service would include more mediation and synthesis than the basic level.

Full: Resource libraries in which the library would contain research level document-based collections and a fuller range of electronic information with the most sophisticated gateways to other electronic information. The collection would be supplemented by the addition of on-campus databases. The level of service would include in-depth mediation. The cost per transaction would be low and the fixed cost high.

WORKING IDEAL NETWORKS

What is needed in these types of networks are the following:

1. The synergy of different networks working together for some time. Since the patterns are still evolving, it is important to try not to harden new definitions too soon. The psychological difficulty we have faced with copyrighting databases is that such hardening seems to have closed our options too early.
2. The continued pooling of resources in formal networks in order to support such synergy and to produce the following:
   a. Staff who can do research and development. We must explore the future more actively with some bit of venture capital.
   b. To some degree, the testing of developed products to determine their fit with bimodal, dualistic library programs-again a bit of venture capital can be invested in this—with some degree of competition existing.
   c. Broad thinking about communications mechanisms and telecommunications networks, with overall design of gateways, etc.
   d. Broad thinking about new kinds of bibliographic access. I am not so much interested in AACR3 as I am in the combining of various types of information resources into one system in order to meet my own needs and the needs of surrounding, but smaller libraries.
   e. The consideration of entirely new budget models for the use of the tax dollar, and private giving within the certain context of providing information and dealing with the federal deficit at the

same time. Open access as an ethical and social issue is something we must continue to address.

f. A concentration on *integration* even as we consider diversification and differentiation. For surely I am willing to experiment with ten new CD-ROM products depending upon the type and size of my library, but in the end what I am looking for is integration and linkage — how can my library as an information system provide integrated access to all kinds of information resources? What is the critical mass of programs and products which I can maintain in order to provide such integrated access? And here, I believe, is a role which can be strongly played by libraries and networks of libraries which is somewhat difficult for the private sector — integration both with my systems and with my programs.

g. Definitions of roles for comprehensive information systems, selective information systems, and highly tailored information systems — for the full service resources, the intermediate services and the basic services. These are areas in which we spend too much money to make a lot of mistakes — unlike some of the venture capital areas.

h. Continuing discussion of lead time. It is the case now, that it takes considerable time and money to get the staff and equipment in place to provide access to electronic information at the same time that we continue to provide access to document based collections. How can we together discuss, consider, and plan for such lead time in a way in which group discussions benefit the individuals?

i. And finally, that we consider the tradeoffs between size of network and the critical mass required to have the momentum and the clout to get things done as opposed to the benefits of likemindedness that can come with smaller subsets of our networks. We will simply wear a lot of hats for some time and continue to juggle them with even more dexterity.

FURTHER STRATEGIES

1. Use both short- and long-term strategies;
2. Define and test assumptions within the network. Look for subsets of assumptions for subsets of the network and for individual libraries;
3. Develop a series of questions to insure the right answers: What have been the resources shared? Who have been the sharers?

Who created the resources? What has been the philosophy/ethics of sharing? What have been the economics of resource-sharing? At which levels has value been added? What shifts are occurring? At what levels of resource-sharing are they occurring? Where has vertical and/or integrative thinking had influence? What is the nature of real-world negotiation, the psychology of consultation, and the nature of leadership in the knowledge environment? What is the nature of librarianship as a gestalt, what is the user gestalt? Is the nature of information support systems which exist to create synergy through bringing together human minds with the records left by other human minds changing?

In considering resource-sharing systems, all of the above questions also imply a series of questions related to the type, subject, scope, quantity, and availability of existing and/or potentially deriveable data and information relevant to the needs of the particular information environment: What types of organized information exist or may exist in the near future which will be potentially useful (valuable) for the tasks and problems of that environment? How are the data organized? How are they packaged? What is their cost? How can they be acquired or accessed and what is the lead time? Who are the information suppliers in these areas of concern? What, if any, are restrictions on use? Are there any other specific constraints? Are there specialty consulting firms that provide a knowledge base in the field? How can the information be integrated with the present information systems in the library? How can the information be delivered individually or through networks or through other telecommunications? Does this require venture capital or non-venture capital and what are the risks involved? What "make or buy" decisions are feasible and possible?

4. Develop a set of positions on information policy.

NOTE

1. Philip H. Mirvis and David Berg, eds. *Failures in Organization Development and Change.* (New York: Wiley, 1977.)

Balancing Needs: The Ideal Network of the Future

Susan K. Martin

INTRODUCTION

For the purposes of this discussion, I will define networks as those organizations whose primary activity is to provide electronic bibliographic information to libraries, either directly or by contract with another organization. Automated library networks were nonexistent in the 1960s: with the pressure upon OCLC to provide services outside the state of Ohio in the 1970s, the OCLC management made a decision which has had enormous ramifications upon libraries and the way they operate. OCLC said that it could not serve individual libraries outside Ohio, but it would be willing to work with *groups* of libraries. The networks were in a large part established as a result of this decision, although many cooperatives pre-existed. Some of these changed their modus operandi to include contracting for OCLC services.

This is a time of major challenge for the regional networks. Any study of networks is likely to say that networks can only succeed if they are perceived as being beneficial to all parties involved. A study conducted in 1973 showed that the chief reason for library directors' involvement in networks was to alleviate the problem of decreasing financial resources.[1] Another researcher indicated that a network and its members must be closely aligned in purpose; otherwise there will be little commitment and loyalty to the network.[2] If these analyses are correct, and I believe they are, the current situation hints of elements of instability.

Susan K. Martin is Director of the Milton S. Eisenhower Library of Johns Hopkins University. She has a BA in Romance Languages from Tufts University and an MA and PhD in Library Science from the University of California, Berkeley. Dr. Martin has published extensively on the subject of networking. This article was presented as a paper at the joint AMIGOS/SOLINET meeting in May, 1987.

© 1988 by The Haworth Press, Inc. All rights reserved.

CONDITIONS FOR SUCCESS

An article by Gillham and Beckman suggests some conditions for success of a network: participation is voluntary; costs and benefits are perceived to be distributed equitably; the central organization only coordinates—it does not control; and standards must be accepted and maintained.[3] Many others have suggested that the keys to a thriving network are the functions which it performs and its ability to fill a real need. A further point which has been solidly embedded in our literature is that made by Barbara Markuson to the effect that networking can only be successful if it is a bottom-up, grass-roots effort; it is not and cannot be imposed from the top down. Moreover, it is local funds that have supported networking to date.[4]

What does this tell us? Most of these thoughts were offered in the 1970s and early 1980s. Has time made a difference in the way a successful network evolves and functions? I would suggest that, technical details aside, the basic principles still apply. We have not examined these principles for a number of years—there was a spate of discussion of networks in the mid-1970s, but not since then—and it is probably well worth our time and effort now to re-examine these issues. Do librarians still participate in networks in an effort to deal with constrained financial situations? Is there any other reason to belong to a network? Probably there is, and the answer relates to the questions of networks filling member needs and being mutually beneficial.

I suggest that the two prongs upon which today's successful network and possibly tomorrow's ideal network rests are financial relief and functional benefit. Networks will survive and perhaps flourish if it is perceived that the benefits they offer outweigh the costs. Before we can discuss tomorrow's ideal network, we need to look at these two forces in the light of today's situation. My perception of instability in the system of networks is directly related to the way in which libraries perceive and accommodate financial constraints and functional benefit, and what I see as an increasing willingness to explore achievement of goals by using mechanisms which do not fall within the traditional categories of library cooperation; i.e., commercial services are what Henriette Avram refers to as "an erosion of sharing."

In the late 1980s, networking is now approaching a watershed. Local online systems are increasingly available, not only for the large affluent libraries but also for smaller institutions. In addition, the private sector is creating and offering products which compete with the networks and utilities, and they are able to offer very attractive prices because they focus on general needs. In at least one important way, the local systems of today are unlike the batch punched card systems of the 1960s and early 1970s: they cost much more and therefore are often balanced by the library against the costs of networking, which can also be significant. Library administrators are beginning to weigh the costs and benefits of belonging to networks and using bibliographic utilities, as opposed to investing in a local system and using commercial products. If an integrated local system is judged to be not only necessary but also of higher value than network membership, that network may go by the board. Or, more likely, the library will remain a member of the network but not take advantage of its services, thereby eliminating the revenues that its budget formerly provided the network. This situation has a paradoxical quality: the network manager and governing body may not be able to foresee a simultaneous increase in membership and decrease in services and therefore revenues.

Let me ask you to consider the various options available to you if all you want to do is to acquire bibliographic data. Particularly in smaller libraries, LC/MARC records from whatever source are likely to fulfill that particular need. Why, then, join a network? The LC records are available from the private sector, and of course from LC itself at a very low price. What is missing? Interlibrary loan, among other things. One could surmise that it is essential to retain networks because they present the only mechanism we have for communicating holdings information and ILL requests. I suggest that this reason alone is not sufficient; we may need to retain a bibliographic data base with holdings information—an online NUC, but we may not need the existing cooperative structure, including regional networks, to do so.

RECENT PERCEPTIONS AND STRUCTURES

The world is changing around us, and is doing so rapidly. This thought seems trite and obvious, but it is remarkable that so often we do not take it into consideration when attempting to deal with an issue. We cannot assume that the values and systems held in reverence by the library profession in the past will retain the same status in the future. Two very important statements have been made recently, statements which have the potential of affecting networking in the future.

First, the Library of Congress' Network Advisory Committee (NAC), which has spent the past year examining the networking structure and setting an agenda for the future, stated that a physical national data base was impossible to achieve, and that networking efforts would focus on linking systems to provide a *logical* national network.[5]

Those who have been observers of networks for the past ten years or more should not be surprised; the statement does not seem to be startling, outrageous, or even new. But it is important to note that it is new, in a sense. It is the strongest statement yet made by this influential national group on an issue which has been debated over the years. Following from the statement one can perceive the establishment of small regional or even local networks, which have the capability of communicating with other networks using the Linked Systems Protocol. I doubt that there will be a rush away from OCLC and toward smaller networks, but in an indirect manner the NAC statement tells the profession that this approach would be acceptable.

A second recent statement which portends interesting developments for the future came from OCLC. A report at an OCLC Users' Council meeting indicated that OCLC management perceives its network members as wanting to continue its traditional services, implying that these members are not interested in exploring different ways of providing the same services or the establishment of new services.[6] You may ask what problem this attitude creates. The primary issue is that OCLC, as RLG, believes that the current structure of a large centralized data base offering services to libraries may not be viable in the future. As an organization, OCLC is ambitious and interested in applications other than the "traditional" bibliographic services; its management therefore perceives that they are bucking the tide of the system users. At the same time they are attempting to protect the organization by becoming involved in exactly the type of system they believe will compete with the network—the local systems. Followers of *Library Hotline* will be aware that there is some potential here for OCLC going forward and leaving its users behind, as OCLC becomes more determined to deal directly with user libraries and not through regional networks.[7]

Let's look for a moment at the bibliographic utilities, casting off the standard perception of them. UTLAS, which has always considered itself to be a commercial vendor, is being bought by another vendor for the second time in just a few years. What do vendors do? They try to generalize their products to allow them to earn as much as possible without spending a great deal to customize their systems and services to each customer.

At one end of the spectrum, this approach is often referred to as "skimming the cream"—taking care of the bulk of the business and paying no attention to that 10-20% of the cases which seem to need customization and special attention. At the other end of the spectrum, we can see a reflection of this approach in OCLC's decision, many years ago, not to offer unlimited varieties of printed cards, but instead to give each user a standard set of options.

OCLC is not a commercial organization in name or in governance structure, but in behavior it is increasingly looking like a vendor. RLG calls itself a partnership, since it is owned by the thirty-six full members, but it faces the same kinds of issues as does OCLC in coping with the technology of today and tomorrow. These three utilities will all suffer from the competition of the private sector if they are not allowed by their boards to develop services which are either now being sold or are being contemplated by the private sector.

For this reason, it is clear that librarians need to be creative about the bibliographic utilities and networks, and not continue to think only in terms of traditional roles. In the future, vendors will offer new information services which will appear to be attractive and cost-effective; librarians will buy those information services. If one accepts this prediction as a given, why not then allow the utilities and networks to explore directions which deemphasize traditional bibliographic processing and support innovative information technologies and tools for the future?

Let me paraphrase: we all resist change, and we tend to characterize the organizations with which we deal in specific, non-changing terms. In the case of utilities and networks, there should probably be suitable planned change for growth and diversity; because they are our organizations and we are their directors or trustees, we have the power to prevent healthy growth as well as to stimulate it. It is my belief that we should practice sound management of our networks as well as of our libraries, and work with network staff to ensure appropriate development of these organizations.

We have a tendency to make decisions which optimize our resources or services in the short run, without considering the long-run implications. To be specific, we may all think that a system of networks is a good idea; but if individually we turn away from network services to commercial services or local systems, we will ultimately destroy the very system we created to suit our needs.

THE IDEAL NETWORK

I do not mean to suggest that all networks and utilities should constantly grow, change, and add services. On the contrary, with the proliferation of local systems, the very existence of some networks may be called into question. Not all networks which have ever been formed continue to exist; networks such as the Five Associated University Libraries (FAUL) and the Mid-Atlantic Research Libraries Information Network (MARLIN) have been voted out of existence by their governing boards. The inertial force, however, leans on the side of the continued existence of organizations, until some circumstance such as the financial condition of the network or apathy of the members causes the chief players to look seriously for other options.

But what is, really, the ideal network of the future? I am not at all sure that it can be defined, except in terms of general characteristics which might be either required or desirable to promote a healthy organization. There are hundreds of networks and consortia in this country, and each has its own traits; each group of member libraries has its own standard for a satisfactorily operating network. For example, AMIGOS and SOLINET have some shared characteristics: they are large, multi-type, and have been able to develop their own technical environments. They are very different from networks such as NE-LINET or MINITEX, which are smaller, have different emphases, and have not created a large technical capacity. Not only are the networks different, but the willingness of the members within any network to participate and to provide financial backing differs vastly from one network to another. As such, it is difficult, if not impossible, to describe *the* ideal network. It may be possible to identify features which are important to the success of such a network, however.

Let us go back to the two primary issues upon which rests the motivation of a library to participate in a network: financial relief and functional benefit. Obviously, the ideal network of the future cannot cost more than its members believe they can afford. Until the advent of costly local systems, the formula for determining affordability could be relatively simple. In fact, at least one study showed that in 1979 a large group of research library directors believed that they could spend as much as four percent of their annual operating budgets on network costs.[8] Let us assume that four percent is still a valid number to use in terms of allocating a portion of the library's operating budget toward automation. As the popularity of local systems grows, that four percent may not increase, but it will be required to accommodate not only the network costs but also the costs of the local system. That is, the pie does not increase without some unusual effort on the part of the library administration *and* unusual understanding of the tradeoffs by the parent organization's administration. For example, without an infusion of new funds or creative use of existing resources, the librarian with a budget of $1 million may be faced with the problem of taking an existing $40,000 for automated services (primarily OCLC) and reallocating it among OCLC, the regional network, and the local system.

The first reaction of many people is that something has to give. Which one shall it be?

That brings us to functional benefit. Among the perceived benefits of networking are:

- resource sharing
- shared cataloging
- ownership of bibliographic data
- access to jointly-owned, centralized data bases (authority files, nonbibliographic files, etc.)
- control of the technological destiny of the library and the profession
- cooperative preservation

One cannot quarrel with these goals. But within the context of describing the ideal network of the future, it will be necessary to identify which of the above benefits can or should be provided by which element: the bibliographic utility, the regional network, the private sector, the individual library, the Library of Congress, or other entities yet to be determined.

Before so doing, however, it will be useful to examine networking *behaviors*, particularly with reference to autonomy or the loss thereof. Much has been said about autonomy, with most commentators believing that librarians are concerned about loss of control (certainly the response to the OCLC copyright of the data base would support this conclusion).[9] In a paper written at a time of good fiscal health in libraries, De Gennaro identified two interrelated problems as being loss of autonomy, and dependence upon an uncontrollable remote organization. He asserted that distributed systems linked to nationwide data bases would alleviate both problems.[10] Huntington Carlile believed that librarians support local and regional cooperative efforts, but are fearful of so-called cooperative structures at the national level.[11]

I suggest that the ideal for many librarians is that their libraries be sufficiently affluent to be able to serve all internal and patrons' needs without reliance on outside agencies. Defined in the extreme, this status would mean that every requested book would already be in the collection, and that the library would have adequate staffing to fully catalog every item. This end of the spectrum has never been reality for most of us; even libraries such as the Library of Congress or the New York Public Library cannot attempt to achieve this kind of self-sufficiency.

The next notch as we move across this spectrum is the ability to pay for everything purchased or contracted for externally, and at the same time to develop local systems, whether automated or not, to suit the needs of the staff and users of the library. It is this scenario with which we are not grappling; the outcome of the struggle will determine the nature of the future network. Some historical background should put this situation into perspective: in the 1960s, libraries created their own automated systems, which were usually batch processing systems. In the early 1970s, OCLC made its online services publicly available, and within a very few years thousands of libraries were using OCLC for cataloging and interlibrary loan. The bulk of OCLC's users signed up for the service in the 1970s; those libraries which did not use OCLC either began to use another utility such as RLIN or WLN, or decided to eschew network participation altogether. Libraries then reduced the size of their cataloging staff, bought terminals and increased their annual budgets to accommodate OCLC tranaction costs and whatever associated regional network costs might be involved. At this time, in 1987, it is unthinkable to go back to the old way of doing business, and it is very difficult to think about replacing OCLC services with a substitute, whether it be a commercial online service or a locally situated CD-ROM. However, the concept of the local online system is intriguing. In fact, it is more than intriguing; it is a concept to which we are gradually being driven by peer pressure, user pressure, and the sense that a local system can finally offer us a way to give our users more access to locally held material.

The current local online systems, however, are much more costly than the batch systems of twenty years ago. Some libraries will manage to expand the pie to pay both a local system and continuing full participation in a network. Others will find it necessary to trade off the benefit of centralized and local automation, and may decide to eliminate existing network services or replace them with alternative, less expensive, sources of information.

I want to return now to the benefits of networking, and suggest a comparison among OCLC, RLG, regional networks (generalized) and the local library (generalized). Table 1 indicates my assessment of the locus of these benefits.

This table reflects the current situation as we have allowed it to develop. Note that strengths are almost evenly divided between utilities and regional networks; this distribution is not an accident, but a consequence of OCLC's early decision not to support libraries outside Ohio. Note also that the private sector's strengths are beginning to match the strengths of the utilities.

While it is not possible to describe the ideal network, it is possible

TABLE 1

Loci of Network Benefits, 1987

Feature	Utility	Private	Regional Networks	Local
Resource sharing	XX		X	
Shared cataloging	XX	XX	X	
Ownership of data	X	X	XX?	XX
Access to databases	XX	X	X	
Control of destiny	X		X	XX
Preservation	X		X?	
Training	XX?	X	XX	X

X=moderate support
XX=strong support
? denotes variability depending on the institution

to describe a set of functions which is needed by the library community at a reasonable cost. Given these functions and their attendant costs, it is up to the librarians, network staff, and utility to modify the existing network structure to suit these needs. Looking at this table, one could imagine a scenario whereby the utilities diminish in importance because the various functions have been taken over by the private sector or the regional networks in conjunction with local systems. It is more likely that regional networks will lose strength, because they are operating from a position of relative weakness. They have insufficient capital, and their status in the eyes of their members is variable; not so the case with OCLC or an RLG. It is possible that a future structure would contain one or more OCLC-like organizations, and regional networks would split up into smaller regional or local groups which can accommodate member needs according to geographic location, type of library, or funding source.

ROLE OF REGIONAL NETWORKS

If my projection is accurate, any one of the existing participants in the network scene can manipulate the system components to strengthen its own role. For regional networks such as AMIGOS and SOLINET, suitable actions would include the following: they should examine stimulating the development of subgroups within the network, to avoid being split up by unforeseen member action; as change agents, they must be flexible, to see what the market wants now and to anticipate what it may want in the future; they must recognize the financial stringencies being placed on libraries because of local systems, and be prepared to offer creative financial or organizational solutions to an almost intractable problem; and they should attempt to work with their governing boards to identify those new information services which libraries *will buy* ultimately from the private sector, to suggest that such programs be undertaken by the network. In both AMIGOS and SOLINET, the latter action has al ready borne fruit, with AMIGOS Shares program and SOLINET's preservation effort.

CONCLUSION

In summary, libraries will continue to cooperate, but networks as we know them today do not have to be the sole mechanism for their doing so. Network and utility staffs will have to think and behave like the private sector in order to offer financially attractive alternatives to their members.

If regional networks continue to exist, they will need to perform as change agents to push librarians to see beyond the traditional services offered by utilities and networks. The major professional decision-makers are no longer members of network boards of directors, thus creating a vacuum which tends to be filled by caution rather than boldness.

The structure of our nationwide system of networks may very well change significantly. There is no longer a striving toward a single nationwide data base; a resulting phenomenon may be the weakening of regional networks and an increase in the number of smaller networks serving like-minded libraries. In New England, for example, NELINET is no longer the only, or even the foremost, network; there are at least five or six networks in that small area alone.

It is essential that librarians work within the coming few years to resolve the tension between networks and local systems. Strong leaders at the network level will be needed to facilitate this change; otherwise, networks will continue to serve only the lowest common denominator.

I would like to leave you with a more positive view for the regional network. I find this view to be difficult, because as you know, libraries are usually poorly funded service units of their parent organizations, and networks constitute secondary, also poorly funded, services. I am sure that, functionally, libraries will acquire the systems they need, whether local or shared, to use new information technologies for the benefit of the users and the libraries themselves. The leaders and managers of regional networks will have to respond to their challenge by assessing the market, and guiding network programs to fit the needs and pocketbooks of network members. The level of positive efforts and the creativity of the network leaders themselves will play the most important roles in determining their own futures.

NOTES

1. Susan K. Martin, *Governance Issues for Automated Library Networks: Impact on, and Implications for, Large Research Libraries*. Diss. University of California, Berkeley, 1982.
2. Wallace C. Olsen, "Networks: Constraints—Jurisdictional and Organizational," in *Networks and the University Library*. Chicago: Association of College and Research Libraries, 1979, pp. 53-56.
3. Virginia Gillham and Margaret Beckman, "Individual Autonomy and Successful Networking: A Canadian Experience," in *New Horizons for Academic Libraries*. New York: K.G. Saur, 1979, pp. 291-295.
4. Barbara E. Markuson, "Revolution and Evolution: Critical Issues in Library Network Development," in *Networks for Networkers*, Blanche Wools and Barbara Markuson, eds. New York: Neal Schuman Press, 1980, pp. 3-28.
5. Article from recent *Hotline*.
6. OCLC Users' Council minutes.
7. "Reading the OCLC Users' Council Meeting Minutes," *Library Hotline*, 16 (April 6, 1987), p. 2.
8. Susan K. Martin, *Governance Issues for Automated Library Networks*, op. cit.
9. Sally Drew, "Online Databases: Some Questions of Ownership," *Wilson Library Bulletin*, (June, 1985), pp. 661-663.
10. Richard De Gennaro, "The Role of the Academic Library in Networking," in *Networks for Networkers*. New York: Neal-Schuman, 1980, p. 304-308.
11. Huntington Carlile, "The Diversity Among Legal Structures of Library Networks," in *Networks for Networkers*. New York: Neal-Schuman, 1980.

For Product Safety Concerns and Information please contact our EU
representative GPSR@taylorandfrancis.com
Taylor & Francis Verlag GmbH, Kaufingerstraße 24, 80331 München, Germany